'Experts Aghast!'

'Experts Aghast!'

March 8—Your friendly fake-news media is now telling you, in regard to President Putin's annual address to Russia's Federal Assembly just one week ago, that "Oh, we knew about it all along—and anyway, it's not true." But in the unguarded early hours right after that speech, they inadvertently let some of the truth slip out. NPR titled a March 1 wire, "Experts Aghast at Russian Claim of Nuclear-Powered Missile with Unlimited Range." They quoted Edward Geist, a researcher specializing in Russia at the Rand Corporation, "I'm still kind of in shock. My guess is they're not bluffing, that they've flight-tested this thing. But that's incredible."

And that's just what *EIR* has confirmed: that the leading Western scientists and Russian specialists who are paid to know about these things, knew nothing. They were completely in the dark.

Now that State of the Nation message of President Putin has many implications, and they're still only just beginning to hit home. First and probably most important, as Helga Zepp-LaRouche has stressed—whatever anyone may imagine otherwise, the "unipolar world" fantasy is dead. The 2016 election of Donald Trump was a body-blow to the notion that American "muscle" would dominate the world militarily in behalf of British "brains," but now it is dead forever.

And then, ask yourself what our intelligence agencies were doing with their untold billions of dollars, besides tapping everyone's phones? In searching for the Russians under our beds and in our White House, they seem to have missed everything of importance about what real Russians have been doing for up to 15 years.

Now move on to some of the most obvious impli-

Russian Ministry of Defense

New Russian hypersonic missile being tested.

cations for space exploration and, bound up within it, for the future of the world economy. Taken as a whole, the final third of President Putin's speech, the part which laid out new weapons systems (especially its closing sentences), made it clear that humanity is within close reach of a nuclear-powered space plane, which would provide vastly better access to space than rockets, the space shuttle, or anything else available today. The original space plane was the brainchild of the late Austrian scientist Eugen Sänger, whose approach was supported by Lyndon LaRouche and such other experts as the late lamented U.S. "astronaut's astronaut," John Young. But a nuclear-powered space plane, which now comes into prospect, is far superior to the conventional fuel-burning designs of the past and present—until we have a fusion-powered space plane. (It is of interest, though, that China flight-tested a scaled-down version of a conventional space plane on March 2.)

How about nuclear power? U.S. Energy Secretary Rick Perry, and also the Canadian government, are trying to progress towards eventual assembly-line production of small modularized nuclear reactors. These will have enormous importance especially for less-developed areas in Asia, Africa, and Ibero-America. But Putin's Russia seems to have the jump on us here as well. President Putin said that Russia had developed a "small-scale heavy-duty nuclear energy unit that can be installed in a missile like ... the American Tomahawk missile. " Anyone happen to know the diameter of a Tomahawk missile? It is 20 inches. He also said that the nuclear energy unit made for Russia's new undersea drone was more powerful than those of their nuclear submarines, while a hundred times smaller.

Two additional advances announced by President Putin bear especially on the drive for fusion power under Lyndon LaRouche's "Four Laws," which are the basis of the LaRouche PAC 2018 campaign. First, although no details were given, there have been advances in lasers. Second, in speaking of the new Mach 20 guided atmospheric delivery vehicle, Putin said, "The use of new composite materials has made it possible to enable the gliding cruise bloc to make a long-distance guided flight practically in conditions of plasma formation." Indeed those conditions at Mach 20 are closely comparable to those in the "fireball" re-entry of the Space Shuttle to earth atmosphere—but the latter can only be sustained for a brief period. Here Putin's remarks seem to indicate that there have been new advances in the physics of the gaseous/plasma shock-front, building on the progress begun in the past by Bernhard Riemann and carried forward later by Ludwig Prandtl, Adolf Busemann and others.

To now sum all this up from a different, cultural point of view: we are now entering into a new period of rapid technological attrition—one different from, and yet in a way comparable to the period from the launching of Sputnik on Oct. 4, 1957, until John F. Kennedy's assassination on Nov. 22, 1963, or somewhat later, when only a minority of our presently living citizens had yet been born.

These issues point to the deeper considerations underlying Lyndon LaRouche's Strategic Defense Initiative and his (and the late Edward Teller's) initiative for the Strategic Defense of the Earth. Those ideas of LaRouche are the basis on which the coming negotiations with Putin's Russia and other nations must be based. Undergirding it all is the truth of the distinction of the human species from all others known.

EIR Contents

www.larouchepub.com Volume 45, Number 11, March 16, 2018

Cover This Week

Artist's depiction of Russian hypersonic missile from Vladimir Putin's March 1 Presidential Address to the Federal Assembly.

ZEPP-LAROUCHE WEBCAST

The Strategic Shift Inherent in Putin's 'Sputnik Shock'

This is the edited transcript of the March 9, 2018 Schiller Institute New Paradigm webcast interview with the founder of the Schiller Institutes, Helga Zepp-LaRouche. She was interviewed by Harley Schlanger. A video of the webcast is available.

Harley Schlanger: Hello. I'm Harley Schlanger from the Schiller Institute. Welcome to our international webcast today with Helga Zepp-LaRouche, who is the founder of the Schiller Institutes.

Helga, at the beginning of this year, you issued a call for an end to geopolitics, especially geopolitics based on the unilateralist world view of the neo-conservatives and the British imperial doctrine. Events in the last few days have been really quite striking in moving in that direction. People who do not know how to think outside of the box of the geopoliticians have been caught off guard, but you haven't. You and your husband have always been thinking outside that box.

I think we should start with the really amazing development yesterday outside the White House with South Korea's security chief announcing the upcoming summit between Kim Jung-Un and President Trump. Let's begin there in looking at these really incredible changes.

Helga Zepp-LaRouche: I think this is a really groundbreaking development. Hopefully, this meeting between the leader of North Korea, Kim Jung-Un, and President Trump, now planned for May, can overcome the crisis and it can be replaced by economic development and denuclearization of the Korean peninsula. Chung Eui-yong, South Korea's national security ad-

North Korean leader Kim Jong Un (pictured) "stressed his eagerness to meet President Trump as soon as possible," South Korea's national security adviser Chung Eui-yong said. | STR/AFP/Getty Images

Trump meeting with Kim could signal major thaw in nuclear standoff

The surprise announcement came after more than a year of trading threats and insults with the North Korean leader.

viser and Suh Hoon, director of South Korea's National Intelligence Service met with their American counterparts in Washington, and with President Trump. Following that meeting, Chjung Eui-yong announced that in their visit to North Korea following the Olympics, Kim Jung-Un agreed to meet with President Trump. The North Koreans also agreed to not only freeze nuclear weapons tests, but also to halt North Korean missile testing. They also agreed, that for now, the U.S.-South Korean military exercises will continue. This is a major concession. North Korea would be willing to denuclearize if its security is guaranteed. This is their key demand. that North Korea's security must be guaranteed. I think this example should teach people a lesson that President Trump once again outflanked his critics. If that historic meeting were to move forward as planned in the coming two months, one of the most dangerous crisis spots on this planet could be pacified.

I think the desire of the North Korean and South Korean people to unify is motivating these developments. I personally think that in light of the geopolitical manipulation with the deployment of the THAAD missiles in South Korea, people in the two Koreas realized that they were pawns on a geopolitical chessboard. If it would ever come to war, a lot of people—millions and millions of people—in the Koreas would die. This realization has created a very promising development. As we know, there were back-channel discussions involving Russia, China, the United States—who have always had back-channel discussions with North Korea. Just a couple of days ago, President Trump gave lavish praise to China for having played the most important role in bringing this result about.

This is really something extremely important and very positive: it is a model for the cooperation of the three largest powers in the world—the United States, China, and Russia—a model of cooperation to defuse geopolitical crises. That is a very important step in the right direction.

Schlanger: Just to add to that point, I think the critics of Trump have missed the fact that the whole idea of opening to Russia and China is precisely so that this overcoming of geopolitics could take place. You've been very outspoken on the importance of Trump's initiatives in this way, but also I think it's important that the neo-cons who are now attacking Russia and China nonstop—I don't think they'll learn the lesson, but maybe this is the opportunity to sweep them out of the debate.

Russian President Vladimir Putin, at his address to the Federal Assembly, March 1, 2018.

Russian hypersonic Zircon missile set to go into production in 2018.

Zepp-LaRouche: Well, the debate is slowly picking up on what we discussed last week in this program, namely the rather groundbreaking speech which President Putin gave to both houses of the Russian Parliament on March 1. In the last part of this speech, he announced the existence of new weapons systems, a nuclear-powered cruise missile that has almost unlimited reach, which apparently is already deployed, according to some experts, an intercontinental missile with a speed of Mach 20—20 times the speed of sound—which is also unmatched in the West, and nuclear-powered, very fast underwater drones, and laser weapons.

I must say, I've seldom seen—one has seen it on one other occasion—such complete misjudgment by the West. I think I mentioned last week the absolutely ridiculous *Bild Zeitung* German tabloid, which said this speech by Putin was a mouse which squeaked at the lion—meaning the United States—saying this is all completely bluff and doesn't exist. Now, about one week later, it has dawned on some people that indeed, what Putin said at the end of his speech is a reality: He said this now forces the West to the negotiating table, which they have refused to do over the last 16 years. That's certainly interesting: those 16 years were basically the two terms each, of Bush and Obama.

There have been many commentators acknowledging the fact that this has completely changed the balance. Immediately after Putin's speech, you had an analyst from the Rand Corporation—Mr. Geist—who said that this was absolutely incredible, that he was still in shock. The fact that the West was caught completely by

Ronald Reagan Library

President Reagan delivering his speech to the nation on the Strategic Defense Initiative, March 23, 1983.

Taskforce on National and Homeland Security, has a rather hysterical article about that, but he acknowledges that Russia has gained the upper hand in the field of nuclear weapons. However, he calls for a new "Star Wars" against Russia—which is not the way to go about it. It's now 35 years since President Reagan, on March 23, 1983, made his famous speech, declaring the Strategic Defense Initiative (SDI) to be the official policy of the United States. That policy, as many people know, was developed by my husband, Lyndon LaRouche: it was something very different than "Star Wars." We should discuss this further. I think it's now time to revive that proposal.

surprise raises another interesting question: what are all these intelligence services doing? These agencies surveil and spy on every citizen around the globe, looking for Russians under everybody's bed and in the White House, but were completely caught by surprise by this technological military breakthrough by the Russians. Maybe these agencies should be reviewed and their competence should be questioned in Congressional hearings.

A very interesting article by Professor Stephen Cohen, professor emeritus of Princeton and New York University, asks the question: has the West provoked a nuclear arms race, and maybe lost it? He poses this as a question. I think others are also waking up to the reality, for example, Senators Edward Markey (D-Mass.), Jeff Merkley (D-Ore.), Dianne Feinstein (D-Calif.), and Bernie Sanders (I-Vt.) issued an urgent letter to Secretary of State Rex Tillerson, requesting him to begin a new round of strategic talks with Russia following Putin's speech. I think this is very good. Dr. Peter Pry, the executive director of the

Schlanger: I think that's really important. As you said, it's the 35th anniversary coming up in just a little more than a week and a half—March 23, 1983—when Reagan shocked most of the American people by saying he wanted to make an offer to share and collaborate with the Russians (the Soviet Union at the time) the development of an anti-missile defense system. We had been campaigning for that going back to the late 1970s when Lyndon LaRouche wrote his pamphlet, "Sputnik of the Seventies: The Science Behind the Soviets' Beam Weapon."

What I find interesting is that over the years, Lyndon LaRouche's ideas, the work you've done with Russia, and the scientific questions posed there have all been debated and discussed in Russia, while there's been silence on that in the United States. I think if we're going to come to terms with the implications of Putin's statement, people must turn back to what Lyndon LaRouche said leading up to President Reagan's 1983 SDI policy, and then in the period after that.

Zepp-LaRouche: I would strongly urge you, our viewers, to

Lyndon LaRouche's pamphlet issued in the 1970s.

go to the *Executive Intelligence Review* archive and read the article, "Draft Memorandum of Agreement between the United States and the USSR" by my husband, which was first published March 30, 1984 and republished a week ago. I always thought that particular document was one of the most far-sighted and visionary papers of the many, many beautiful papers my husband has written over the decades. This was one year after the SDI was proposed by President Reagan and the counter-reaction to Reagan's SDI policy was incredible. It came from the Bush circles in the Reagan Administration, but it came also from the circles of Marshal Ogarkov in the Soviet military. One year after Reagan's 1983 speech, my husband made this very far-reaching proposal, to basically dissolve the NATO and Warsaw Pact blocs, to instead use the collaboration between NATO and the Warsaw Pact—especially between the United States and the Soviet Union—to develop weapons based on new physical principles; to apply those principles in the civilian sector for a science driver effect; and to use the subsequent increase in the productivity of both the United States and the Soviet Union (but especially in the Soviet economy) for major technology transfers to the developing countries to overcome underdevelopment, instead of turning developing countries into sites for proxy wars between the superpowers. The principles which were laid out in the opening statement of this article are that the political foundation for a durable peace must be the absolute, unconditional sovereignty of all nations, cooperation among sovereign nation-states, and unlimited opportunities to participate in the benefits of technological progress, to the mutual benefit of each and all.

If you read this document today, you can't help but realize that what China is proposing, win-win cooperation and a new model of relations among major powers and all nations, is clearly based on the same principles: access to technology for all, mutual respect for national sovereignty, and non-interference. This is a very beautiful example of the power of ideas: even though these ideas were not acted upon in the short-term, nevertheless they later exerted great influence because these ideas are coherent with the nature of the human species—creativity being the feature which distinguishes mankind from all other species. Then, eventually, these ideas will become dominant. So, while this is not an automatic process—it requires human intervention—

NATO

Czech General Pavel, Chairman of the NATO Military Committee.

nevertheless I think now is the time to do what Foreign Minister Lavrov and President Putin were both calling for—to sit down and discuss a new global security architecture which guarantees the security of all, the United States, Russia, China, Europe, and also smaller nations like the two Koreas and many other countries which still have a lot of problems.

I think it's really the moment for a complete change in the strategic alignment, to create a new global security architecture, and do what my husband proposed with the SDI, to eventually make nuclear weapons technologically obsolete. This curse, which could lead to the extinction of the human species, must really absolutely go away forever.

Schlanger: You mentioned NATO: The shock effects from Putin's speech appear to even have been felt in Brussels, where the Chairman of the NATO Military Committee, General Petr Pavel, said that it is now time to talk with Russia and stop seeing Russia as an aggressor and develop better relations. So, it is clear that these shock effects are being felt everywhere.

Helga, there are also some new developments from China. Foreign Minister Wang Yi gave a press conference which was very far-reaching, which takes up some of these same themes. Why don't you give us a report on what he had to say?

Zepp-LaRouche: This was in the context of the "two sessions," the meetings of the National People's Congress and the Chinese People's Political Consultative Conference which just met in Beijing. Foreign

Shi Mingde, China's Ambassador to Germany featured in the German publication Handelsblatt.

China Foreign Minister Wang Yi speaks in the Great Hall of the People.

Minister Wang Yi gave a press conference in the Great Hall of the People. He said that China is now proposing a completely new model of international relations based on the idea of benefiting all, which includes mutual respect for the sovereignty of other nations. The aim of this is not only the well-being of the Chinese people, but progress for all of humanity. The aim is to create relations among nations such that all the people can have a fulfilled and happy life. He elaborated further, but that is the gist of the idea.

People should really read these things for themselves—that is very important to do—and also take the time to reflect on it. China has, in the last four and a half years—especially with the Belt and Road Initiative, which now reaches into Africa, Latin America, Asia, and Europe—significantly improved international relations. This has improved the relationship among these nations and brought economic benefits to them. It is clear to those who look at these developments that China is not imposing its own model, which unfortunately the negatively oriented and dishonest Western media keeps incessantly repeating.

The Chinese Ambassador to Germany Shi Mingde just wrote a very lengthy article in the German business daily *Handelsblatt* responding to the increased hysteria against China and the New Silk Road being pushed by the Center for Strategic and International Studies (CSIS), which is based in Washington, D.C., and by the German think tank, the Mercator Institute for China Studies (MERICS). It's really a shame, because when these so-called think tanks put out negative propaganda against China, it is sent as press releases, and mainstream journalists—who know nothing about China and don't do their own research—include these dishonest press releases in their articles, which really poison the minds of the readers against China, and against its Belt and Road Initiative, the most important strategic initiative on this planet.

Ambassador Shi Mingde said China has no intention to impose its own model on other nations, and is not doing so. He pointed to the fact that the Belt and Road Initiative is a project for the common good of all people. He pointed out that in 2017 there were 3,673 trains between China and Europe. Forty-eight percent of those trains ended their journey in Germany, pointing to the enormous economic benefit of the trade relations between Germany and China in particular. We urgently need a debate: Why not accept the concept of this Belt and Road Initiative, to overcome geopolitics by aligning the United States, China, Russia, European nations, African nations, Latin American nations, and really work together for win-win cooperation and set a new era of civilization? It's already emerging, but the geopolitical status quo faction of the West is trying to put the brakes on, trying to stop this progress, which is clearly a viable new idea of how the human species can work together. I think we urgently need a public debate about this everywhere.

Schlanger: I don't know if you saw this Helga, but

CC/David Holt

Jeremy Corbyn, British Labour Party leader.

an example of the hysteria you're talking about came when Trump made some remarks at a Republican fundraiser. He talked about his great friendship with Xi Jinping and his respect for him. Then he said, well, you see what Xi did; he just extended his term. Trump said, this sounds like a pretty good thing; maybe we should try it here. The media went crazy, saying this proves Trump wants to be a dictator and he's an authoritarian. But, in fact, Xi's initiative was designed to make sure that the projects that have been undertaken by China to alleviate poverty are actually accomplished, rather than being merely talking points.

There are a couple of other things I want to bring up that I think are quite significant. One is in the United Kingdom, where Mohammed bin Salman, the Crown Prince of Saudi Arabia, is on a gigantic road show to talk about the improvements in human rights in Saudi Arabia. But this was addressed very strongly in the Prime Minister's question time in Parliament by Jeremy Corbyn, the head of the Labour Party, who challenged the British government for its continued role in arming Saudi Arabia, which is committing genocide in Yemen. What can you tell us about this, Helga?

Zepp-LaRouche: I think it's very important, even though Great Britain is not the only country which is continuously supplying Saudi Arabia with weapons. Corbyn importantly said that UK military advisers have been helping Saudi Arabia in targetting civilian sites like schools and hospitals, killing an enormous number of civilians and children. We have said this repeatedly: the genocide taking place in Yemen right now is one of the worst things to have happened in human history. In Germany, during the period of National Socialism under Hitler, perhaps many people didn't know what was happening or the question was often asked: who knew what, and when? But this time, you have the slaughter of a whole people, and the whole world knows about it. All the Western political leaders know about it, but absolutely nothing is being done to stop it. So, I really applaud Mr. Corbyn for having the courage to do that. At this conference, Saudi Prince Mohammed bin Salman is meeting with Theresa May, with the Queen, with Prince Charles, with Prince William and several ministers. He is getting the full red-carpet treatment. It's important that Corbyn said what he said in this way. We should really appeal to people that there must be sanctions against Saudi Arabia. Why do you have to have sanctions against so many countries while the one country which is continuing to commit war crimes is left untouched?

cc/Mattia Luigi Nappi

Luigi de Maio, Vice President of the Italian Chamber of Deputies, and leader of the Five Star Movement.

Schlanger: Another development this week was the elections last Sunday in Italy, in which the insurgency against the establishment continued. What do you see coming out of these elections?

Zepp-LaRouche: It looks like the chances are very high that government formation will be even more difficult than it was in Germany. Berlusconi and Renzi, representing the so-called established parties, lost. The winners were the Five Star Movement and Lega Nord, which will make government formation very difficult. Our Liliana Gorini, the chairwoman of Movisol in Italy, issued a statement stating that the only way to have a successful government is to go forward with Glass-Steagall, which is in the platform of the Five Star Movement and Lega Nord, as well as the idea of a national bank which is in their party programs,. But that is not enough: the entire Four Laws of LaRouche must be implemented. We have, despite our relatively small forces in Italy, a powerful voice offering programmatic content to this government formation. Given the fact that the danger of a financial crash is still, like the sword of Damocles, hanging over the world, an initiative from Italy would be an important intervention in this debate. The world is really at a point where we need a debate on what the future should look like.

Let us briefly come back to this question of the SDI. China and Russia clearly have demonstrated that they both have a vision for the future. In China, President Xi Jinping has a vision for 2050 and probably beyond. President Putin, in Russia, clearly has demonstrated that he has a clear perspective for the future of civilization. The long-time idea of my husband, which I have been also campaigning for, is the idea of a New Paradigm. A New Paradigm of human history really means putting the interests of the human species first, before all national interests, and especially before so-called geopolitical interests.

The common aims of mankind are what Xi Jinping calls a shared community for the one future of humanity, or a community of destiny. I think we have to define these common aims, and really focus our energies on them. The common aims, for example, are not just the SDI to create a system of defensive weapons that would make nuclear weapons obsolete, but also to enlarge it into what is called the Strategic Defense of Earth (SDE). We urgently need all nations to put their scientific capabilities together, to develop technologies to deflect or destroy incoming asteroids, meteorites, and other celestial bodies. We also should move in the direction of pre-warning systems against earthquakes and tsunamis. I think the common aim of overcoming poverty is moving well, at least in China and in the countries which are participating with China in the Belt and Road Initiative. But, we need the same aim also for Europe, which has 90 million poor people and so far, no intention to overcome that. At the November 2017 Schiller Institute conference, we put out a resolution calling upon the European Union to lift its population out of poverty by 2020. I think we urgently need that for the United States. It's a shame that a country like the United States should still have more than 40 million poor people. China is the only country really moving to bring development to poor rural areas, to eliminate poverty by 2020.

There are many frontiers of science we should concentrate on. I think we have to rethink our idea of the character of the human species; the human species is not just earthbound. The space cooperation agreement which was just concluded between China and Russia shows that these two nations are thinking in terms of not only developing villages on the Moon, but also developing nuclear-powered space travel that will completely change mankind's ability to reach other planets. These are all areas of international cooperation, and are much more important than the total waste of spending money to make money, on stock exchanges, or anything like that.

I think we can really shape the world in a human way, but we need a debate. For that, I ask all of you to help us to generate this debate and support the Schiller Institute. I invite you to become members, to help us really initiate a different kind of discussion in all countries on this planet, a discussion which would be worthy of the dignity of the human species. I think we are on the verge of making that all possible with your help.

Schlanger: Well, that's a good way to end this program. I get a lot of communications from people who say, "What can we do to bring this New Paradigm online?" Helga just gave you the answer: Be part of triggering this debate. To do that, we have ample material on the newparadigm.schillerinstitute.com website, which can give you background on what the New Silk Road is, and the Four Laws of LaRouche. Take advantage of this: the strategic situation is shifting very rapidly. Helga and Lyndon LaRouche have been at the center of this for decades. Now it's time for us to have not just an insurgency, but a movement of critical thinkers who have the passion to bring this New Silk Road spirit worldwide.

Thank you for joining us. Helga, thank you again. We'll be back next week.

Zepp-LaRouche: Yes, until next week.

hz.zepp@schiller-institut.de

Is New Jersey America's 'Valley of the Clueless'?

by Diane Sare

March 12—On March 1, 2018, President Vladimir Putin of Russia delivered an extraordinary address, announcing that Russia has moved to restore "parity" in nuclear weapons and defense in the wake of the 2002 United States withdrawal from the 1972 ABM Treaty, and the continued expansion of American and NATO bases right up to Russia's borders in Europe. Putin announced the development of weapons based on new technologies, such as missiles driven by nuclear-powered engines, whose range is virtually limitless, as is their ability to evade anti-ballistic missile systems. In other words, he announced that all of America's and NATO's "new" defense systems, upon which billions of dollars have been spent, are already obsolete.

Equally significant, or more significant in the long run, Putin announced a very ambitious and optimistic program to lift millions more of Russians out of poverty, and to increase life-expectancy (which has risen by seven years since 2000) to over 80. He stressed the importance of nurturing the creativity and great ambitions of the nation's young people through cultural and scientific initiatives, including designing and building new cities with museums and cultural centers, and new, modern transportation systems connecting them.

The future growth of Russia's economy, as Putin intends, is coherent with the One Belt One Road Initiative launched by Chinese President Xi Jinping nearly five years ago, which has already transformed the living standards, not only of millions of Chinese, but millions of other people worldwide, including emphatically on the continent of Africa.

What About New Jersey?

Although a dozen or so New Jersey legislators have visited China over the last few years, whatever they may have learned there does not seem to be affecting the policy debate in New Jersey.

Newly-elected Governor Phil Murphy, formerly of Goldman Sachs, and after that Obama's Ambassador to Germany, is moving rapidly to plunge the state into a new dark age. The two most devastating initiatives from his office are the legalization of recreational marijuana, and the shutting down of three of the four nuclear power plants in the state. This is particularly humiliating for a state which is home to the Princeton Plasma Physics Lab, which has made breakthroughs in research for the development of fusion energy.

cc/Phil Murphy for Governor

New Jersey Governor Phil Murphy, formerly of Goldman Sachs.

Currently, due to massive investments in natural gas, New Jersey gets "only" 39% of its electricity from nuclear power, and about 56% from natural gas. Nuclear power was over 50% before 2012. The local power company PSE&G has been championing legislation to allow a very small rate increase to subsidize the nuclear plants in order to keep them operating. This was scheduled to come up for a vote last year, but Governor Murphy put it off, and is not pushing for it now. Exelon, the owner/operator of the plants, has warned that if the subsidy is not approved, it will cease to maintain the plants, causing them to close. Obviously, this would be a sub-

Nuclear power plant, Salem County, New Jersey.

cc/Doug Kerr

PPPL Communications/Elle Starkman

National Spherical Torus Experiment, Princeton Plasma Physics Lab.

stantial loss of power-supply for the state, and will be still more devastating if there is a move to restore the formerly huge manufacturing and machine-tool capability in New Jersey, as there must be. There will simply be no power available for such activity.

Despite the evidence coming in from the State of Colorado, which legalized recreational marijuana four years ago, Governor Murphy is committed to legalizing pot in New Jersey, and cites not just the revenue but "social justice." In Colorado, marijuana is involved in one of every five fatal car accidents, and pedestrian deaths have increased by 16%. Sixty percent of the new Colorado marijuana shops are in minority neighborhoods, and "emergency poison control calls for children, including toddlers, are up 150%."

Are N.J. Officials Already High?

The already horrific state of the local infrastructure has been referenced before in *EIR*. During a recent heavy snow-

YouTube

Denver, Colorado Marijuana Festival, 2014.

storm, two major highways—Routes 280 and 287—were somehow not plowed, resulting in over 530 accidents and over 1,000 calls from trapped drivers, during just a 15-hour period.

Further, it should also be noted that New Jersey Transit has thus far failed to comply with installation of Positive Train Control technology on every commuter car for safety. For that reason, as of Dec. 31, Manhattan's Penn Station, whose tracks are run by Amtrak, will not allow NJ Transit trains to cross the Hudson River. Amtrak has told passengers that they can switch to Amtrak trains on the New Jesey side of the river—but what a mess!

Perhaps Governor Murphy thinks that if we all smoke a little weed, we won't notice that we are freezing in the dark, while stuck in our driveways!

Hello, all fellow New Jerseyans, and all Americans, for that matter! Look at China and Russia! Life doesn't have to be this way! Isn't it time that you listened to LaRouche?

BOOK REVIEW

The Alcibiades Trap: The Stupidity of Anglo-American Arrogance

by Gerry Rose

Destined for War: Can America and China Escape Thucydides' Trap? by Graham T. Allison, with an introduction by Henry Kissinger.

The "Thucydides Trap" thesis has become a very influential way of considering an approach to war avoidance with China. The phrase "Thucydides Trap" was coined by Graham Allison, and the book in question here is the one which made this phrase famous. Allison purports to demonstrate that war is almost always the inevitable outcome when a rising power reaches a point of economic and military strength such that it challenges the hegemony of the existing dominant power. Allison coined the term "Thucydides Trap" from Thucydides' *History of the Peloponnesian War*, which describes the decades-long conflict between Athens and Sparta.

The basis for the book was a project run by Harvard's Belfer Center, which examined sixteen cases since the year 1500 in which a rising power eclipsed an entrenched power. In twelve cases this led to war, and in four cases it did not. Allison's mentor, as he discussed it at a Harvard seminar at the releasing of his book, is Henry Kissinger. So,

U.S. Navy/Zach Allan
Graham Allison

the Thucydides Trap thesis, as a strategic doctrine, has the authority of both Kissinger and Harvard University.

The first time I ran into this thesis was in a report by General Martin Dempsey, then Chairman of the Joint Chiefs of Staff, which referenced it by name at a Carnegie Endowment event. Dempsey was warning President Obama not to get into a war provocation with China simply to maintain American dominance in Asia. General Dempsey put it in this way: The Thucydides Trap "goes something like this—it was Athenian fear of a rising Sparta that made war inevitable. Well, I think that one of my jobs as the chairman of the Joint Chiefs, and as an advisor to our senior leaders, is to help avoid a Thucydides trap. We don't want the fear of an emerging China to make war inevitable. So, Thucydides—so, we're going to avoid Thucydides' trap." This was a very sane view of war with China. General Dempsey was very clear that a dialogue with the People's Liberation Army (PLA) was imperative.

This made sense to me. General Dempsey was warning the Obama administration that, despite the reality that China was on the rise, war was something to be avoided. Given

Obama's narcissistic insanity, it was a very welcome voice of reason in an otherwise insane administration.

The Thucydides Trap thesis is also the terms of reference for war avoidance for both the current National Security Advisor H.R. McMaster, Secretary of Defense James Mattis and even Steve Bannon. Allison starts his book with an anecdote referencing a meeting in the office of then head of the CIA, David Petraeus, where he briefed Petraeus on the insights he had gained into China by his interviews with Lee Kuan Yew, the Prime Minister of Singapore for three decades. Lee was one of Asia's most venerated advisors to both Deng Xiaoping and Xi Jinping, and it is clear that both Kissinger and Allison are knowledgeable about the diplomacy of the region.

Many have accepted the legitimacy of the Thucydides Trap analysis. Even China's *Global Times* has chimed in, stating that the Thucydides Trap warns us

DoD/Sun L. Vega
General Martin Dempsey, former Chairman of the Joint Chiefs of Staff.

DoD/Cherie A. Thurlby
Gen. David Petraeus

DoD/Navy Mass Communication Specialist
1st Class Kathryn E. Hold
Defense Secretary James Mattis

Xinhua/Yin Bogu
Lt. Gen. H.R. McMaster

that there is a real danger of war, and that relations with respect to China and America must be handled wisely. On the other hand, Chinese President Xi has been much more insightful, stating that "There is no such thing as the Thucydides Trap," but only an environment where "major nations time and again make mistakes of strategic miscalculation, and create such a trap for themselves." President Xi was explicitly referring to the current Belt and Road Initiative, where major nations, the United States included, are making a "strategic miscalculation."

Let me be clear. There is a very deep epistemological flaw in Allison's and Kissinger's entire thesis and method. In fact, it is this devastating flaw that provoked me to write this review. It jumps out at anyone familiar with the period of the 19th Century and the rise of the American influence. By reducing each instance of warfare to an individual case, in isolation from the pro-

found systemic changes caused by Alexander Hamilton's anti-imperial economic discoveries, what you are left with is a blatantly fraudulent argument that completely misses the point. This glaring axiomatic error can not possibly be a result of mere incompetence. It is an evil of a certain sophisticated type. As Herr Kissinger is well aware, all of the wars of the 19th and 20th Centuries were caused by the British reaction to the global influence and spread of Hamiltonian economic methods throughout the world. To miss this—or to deliberately omit it—is to miss everything important.

This type of flaw is not new in the history of science. A ground-breaking study, conducted by a scientific research team under Lyndon LaRouche's direction, on the work of Johannes Kepler, gets at the same principle in a clear, devastating way. In the team's work on Kepler's fundamental breakthrough on Universal Gravitation, there is a very stunning account of how all the other systems—of Ptolemy, Copernicus, and Brahe—merely *described,* in one way or the other, what the *appearance* of the orbits of the different planets were. Ptolemy, for instance, used epicycles to explain the orbits and their relationships to the Earth. All three, each with their different schemes, using the same kinds of data, were only able to describe the appearance. It was left to Kepler to investigate the causality.

It is the same with the Thucydides Trap. Yes, indeed, there were sixteen cases from more modern examples, in which a rising power eclipses an entrenched power. Yet, as this article shall detail, the underlying *causes* for war are on a much deeper level. It is actually what might be described as the "Alcibiades Trap," not the Thucydides Trap.

So Far So Good

A couple of details jump out as you read Allison's book. First there is an accurate description, in the beginning of the book, of what China has achieved. In several charts from the chapter, "The biggest player in the history of the world," the book makes several startling comparisons between China in the 1980s and China in 2014. It also compares these differences in China with the United States.

- In 1980 China's GDP was 7% of the U.S. GDP; in 2014 it was 61%.
- In 1980 China's imports were 8% of the U.S.A.; by 2014, they rose to 73%.
- In 1980 China's exports were 8% of the U.S.A.; by 2014, they rose to 141%.
- In 1980 China's foreign reserves were 16% of the U.S.A.; in 2014 they were an unbelievable 3,140%.

While the comparison is stunning, Allison points out further that in total terms of production, China is now already the largest producer in the world of ships, steel, aluminum, clothing, furniture, textiles, cell phones, and computers.

In another chart, projecting into the future, it gets even more interesting. In comparing China's GDP and U.S. GDP:

- In 2004 China had a $5,709 billion GDP; the U.S.A.

Xinhua

College students at a job fair in Hangzhou, China.

had $12,275 billion.
- In 2014 China had a $18,220 billion GDP; the U.S.A. had $17,393 billion.
- By 2024 China is projected to have $35,596 billion GDP; the U.S.A. $25,093 billion.

The book goes on to detail that China will graduate 1.3 million students in science and mathematics, compared to the United States graduating 300,000. China has the largest R&D budget in the world. China already has the fastest computer in the world, along with the largest radio telescope.

The book quotes from many western leaders such as former Prime Minister Rudd of Australia, and others, and makes the point that it is just wishful thinking that this miracle will at all subside. If anything, by 2050 the Chinese economy will be four times that of the United States.

With the evidence of the Chinese economic miracle that Alison provides, the obvious question should be: "What has China done right, and what are we doing wrong?" However, that topic is *verboten* for Allison and Kissinger.

Kissinger and Allison Get It Wrong!

After presenting his evidence of the Chinese economic miracle, Allison tries to make an analogy to Thucydides' *Peloponnesian War,* and it is here that he makes a fundamental *axiomatic* blunder. Yes, Thucydides does say from the very beginning of his history that the cause of the war between Athens and

Sparta was, indeed, the eclipsing by Athens of Sparta, which was then the dominant power in Greece. That fact was argued explicitly by the Corinthians, Sparta's erstwhile ally. They argued that sooner or later there would be a war and that the Spartans would be in a worse position if they did not declare the war right then and there.

Yet Allison, as would be the case for any Kissinger student, entirely misses that this so-called "Trap," as described by Thucydides, only applies when two *oligarchical powers* clash over who will be hegemonic. The current leadership of China has made the point, repeatedly, that under no circumstances do they want to be hegemonic and replace one hegemon with another. The struggle for hegemony is rooted in the very oligarchical system itself, and the war which Thucydides describes falls within that oligarchical matrix.

The key to Thucydides' treatment of the Peloponnesian War, is a section from that work called the *Melian Dialogue*. Allison even quotes the critical message delivered by the Athenian ambassador to the Melians: "We [Athenians] shall not trouble you with specious pretenses.... You know as well as we do that right is a question that only has meaning in relations between equals in power. In the real world the strong do what they will and the weak must suffer what they must." That is the oligarchical outlook, one based on sheer might. What Allison neglects to point out is that the Melians fought heroically, and as their punishment for fighting, the Athenians put to death every male in Melos. This massacre was immortalized by Euripides, the Athenian tragedian who hated the war, in his play *Hecuba*, where he details the same type of massacre of the Trojans by the Greeks as was displayed in the massacre of the Melians. The point to be made is that imperial Athens had become an immoral disgusting abomination.

The immorality which overtook Athens was identical to the moral disease which dominated Sparta. This is defined precisely by Friedrich Schiller, in his insights into Sparta in his essay, *The Legislation of Lycurgus and Solon*. Unfortunately, both Kissinger and Allison have made a living by avoiding such profound insights. Kissinger's scribbling about the Congress of Vienna, *A World Restored*, asserts the view that morality has no place in politics. In this, he is at best Kantian. He concedes that there may be such a thing as morality, but it is unknowable in any sufficient way to act on it. As weak mortals, we can only act to negate heteronomy, i.e., the "negation of negation." There may be universal truths, and we may know them as a *feeling*, but they are

Kai Mörk

Dr. Henry A. Kissinger

unknowable in any scientific way. The awful result of such a mindset is that—for Kissinger and Allison—the idea that there is a new paradigm emerging, one which goes beyond geopolitics and functions on an entirely different orientation toward mankind's future, is inconceivable. For them, only some kind of "cold war" is possible. Only the management of conflicts between new powers eclipsing entrenched powers is possible. Xi Jinping's philosophy of Win-Win, to them, is an unknowable construct. This is the basis for the "Strategic Miscalculation" that President Xi is referring to.

The Alcibiades Trap: The Deeper Truth

We have no greater insight into the Peloponnesian war than the Platonic dialogue *Alcibiades*. It might shock you to know that the two men who founded Western civilization, Socrates and Plato, were violent opponents of the Peloponnesian War. In some sense, the disaster that struck Athens in the wake of Athens' devastating defeat in that war, inspired Plato to inspire Athenians, in perhaps the most profound way in history, to rethink the basis for Government. Plato wrote many of his dialogues attacking the very sophistry which had led Athenian Democracy to war. Also, in the *Alcibiades* dialogue and in the *Republic*, he defines the necessary moral character for leadership. It is the deeper comprehension of Plato's insight that gives us the key to avoid the Thucydides Trap today.

"*Destruction of the Athenian Army in Sicily.*"

H. Vogel

It was well known that Socrates, Euripides and Plato opposed the Peloponnesian war. Euripides was almost killed by the Athenian democracy for producing his plays *Hecuba* and *Iphigenia at Aulis*. In *Iphigenia at Aulis,* Euripides demonstrates the absolute horror of human sacrifice that the Greeks had to commit in order mollify the Olympian gods and to launch the Trojan War. In *Hecuba* he details the unbelievable inhumanity of what was done by the Greeks to Troy in the wake of that city's defeat. It was clearly understood by the Athenians of that time that these were no mere historic curiosities but polemics against the current war and, explicitly, against the horror that was committed against Melos. It was even said that Socrates had written some of the sections of Euripides' plays.

There is critical background to the *Alcibiades* dialogue. The most disastrous adventure of the whole war was known as the Sicilian Expedition, which was launched by Alcibiades. Every Athenian reading the *Alcibiades* dialogue would know that. The dialogue was written more than a decade after the end of the war. It was the Sicilian expedition which was the beginning of the end that brought utter ruin to Athens. Alcibiades argued forcefully for the invasion of Sicily, which swayed the 'Athenian Democracy' to vote to invade Sicily under the guise of treaties with allies on that territory. The expedition was a thinly veiled attempt to increase the Athenian Empire in the midst of the war with Sparta. It is in the nature of Empire that Athens would have to aggrandize itself, to awe other Empires like Sparta and Persia. That was Alcibiades' explicit argument. Sparta and Persia would never expect such audacity, and the invasion would gain their respect. If carried out and successful, all of the Greek states would join Athens.

As it turned out, the expedition was a total failure, in which some 20,000 or more Athenians and their allies were massacred (an enormous amount for that time), and most of their fleet was destroyed. The Athenian commanders were put to the sword, and the 7,000 soldiers who remained alive were sold into slavery. No Athenian could possibly *not know* what Plato was referring to in the *Alcibiades* dialogue.

Plato sets the dialogue *before the disaster* and sets it just as Alcibiades is about to enter the arena for the first time, to sway the Athenian democracy to his will and to take leadership of Athens. It begins with Socrates telling Alcibiades that he has kept watch over him, and the

Gods have bid him to break his silence and speak. Alcibiades was of the noblest family and was trained by Pericles, the original spokesman for the Peloponnesian War.

The dialogue starts with the obvious irony, in which Socrates proves to Alcibiades that he has no idea of what Justice is. Through a series of questions about knowledge and what knowledge is, Socrates shows Alcibiades that his views are based only on opinion. Yet opinion about Justice, which Socrates draws out of Alcibiades, is unlike steering a boat, or mending a shoe. He has no assurance that what he believes is true. In fact, as Socrates demonstrates, nothing is more in dispute than the nature of Justice. In steering a boat, you do know if the man at the tiller is competent or not. In medicine, you know the same. There is a certain type of knowledge which is communicable with knowable results. So how would a 20-year-old youth plan to lead Athens in the making of war and peace? Socrates draws out of Alcibiades that the very subject of war and peace resides in the idea of Justice, of which he has no knowledge. He only has opinion.

Socrates: *I do not suppose that you ever saw or heard of men quarreling over the principles of health and disease to such an extent as to go to war and kill one another for the sake of them.*

Alcibiades: *No indeed.*

Socrates: *But quarrels about justice and injustice, even if you have never seen them, you have certainly heard from many people, including Homer; for you have heard of the Iliad and the Odyssey?*

Alcibiades: *To be sure, Socrates.*

Socrates: *A difference of just and unjust is the argument of those poems.*

Alcibiades: *True.*

Socrates: *Which difference caused all the wars and deaths of Trojans and Achaeans and the deaths of the suitors of Penelope in their quarrel with Odysseus.*

Alcibiades: *Very true.*

Socrates: *…But can they be said to understand that about which they are quarreling to the death?*

Alcibiades: *Clearly not.*

Socrates: *And yet whom you thus allow to be ignorant are the teachers to whom you are appealing.*

The dialogue shifts to the real subject in which Socrates demonstrates a different species of knowledge.

Socrates: *Let me make an assertion which will, I think, be universally admitted.*

Alcibiades: *What is it?*

Socrates: *That a man is one of three things.*

Alcibiades: *What are they?*

Socrates: *Soul, body, or both together forming a whole.*

Alcibiades: *Certainly.*

Socrates: *…But since neither the body, nor the union of the two, is man, either man has no real existence, or the soul is the man?*

Alcibiades: *Just so.*

Socrates: *…..And that is what I was saying before—that I, Socrates, am not arguing or talking with the face of Alcibiades, but the real Alcibiades; or in other words, with his soul.*

Socrates goes on to prove that the soul rules the body.

Socrates: *But he who cherishes his money, cherishes neither himself nor his belongings but is in a stage yet further removed from himself?*

Socrates: *…The reason was that I loved you for your own sake, whereas other men love what belongs to you; and your beauty, which is not you, is fading away, just as your true self is beginning to bloom. And I will never desert you, if you are not spoiled and deformed by the Athenian people; for the danger which I most fear is that you will become a lover of the people and will be spoiled by them. Many a noble Athenian has been ruined in this way.*

…

Socrates: *…Have we not made an advance? For we are at any rate tolerably well agreed as to what we are (the soul) and there is no longer any danger, as we once feared, that we might be taking care not of ourselves, but of something which is not ourselves.*

Alcibiades: *That is true.*

Later on in the dialogue, Socrates makes the point, "But if we have no self-knowledge and no wisdom, can we ever know our own good and evil?"

Socrates goes on making it clear that without know-

The drunken Alcibiades interrupting the Symposium.

Pietro Testa

ing yourself, i.e., "Your soul," it is impossible to know what belongs to *you* and what does not. Further, if you do not know what belongs to you, you cannot know what belongs to others. "And if he knows not the affairs of others, he will not know the affairs of State? And such a man can never be a Statesman?" Socrates continues to prove that without self-wisdom and knowledge there is misery, because of the inability to solve problems, and this leads States to make terrible mistakes. He then tells Alcibiades, "You have not therefore to obtain power or authority, in order to enable you to do what you wish for yourself and the state, but justice and wisdom." Finally with great irony the dialogue ends after Socrates details the nature of freedom, which is based only on virtue, and of slavery, which is Vice and Ruin.

> Socrates: *And are you now conscious of your own state? …And do you know how to escape out of a state which I do not even like to name … by the help of God …*
>
> Alcibiades: *Strange but true; and hencefor-ward I shall begin to think about justice.*

Socrates ends with an incredible irony:

> *And I hope you will persist; although I have fears, not because I doubt you; but I see the power of the state, which may be too much for both of us.*

So it is the corruption of the *Demos* (the People) that will be end of Alcibiades.

Is Morality Knowable?

Since the essence of the politics of war and peace is the question of Justice, and only the soul is capable of knowing Justice, then the real question to be asked is: Is there a scientific standard by which you can judge such questions?

The Alcibiades Trap rules out such questions entirely—thereby leading to the Kantian outlook, which is to strive to avoid bad consequences by negating our fundamental bestial instinct to rule over each other. In Immanuel Kant's *Perpetual Peace,* he argues that only the rule of law prohibits us from our otherwise bestial instincts. "The state of peace among men living side by side is not the natural state; the natural state is one of war." This is the mindset of Kissinger and his *epigone*, the imperial notion of British geopolitics. Imperialism claims that the Idea, which is the preamble to our Declaration of Independence, of "Life, Liberty, and the Pursuit of Happiness," is perhaps, a nice ideal, but ultimately chimerical and unknowable. The geopoliticians put the concept of the "General Welfare" in the U.S. Constitution into the same category—All we are capable of doing is prohibiting ourselves from killing each other. So the principle of *Win-Win*, or as Xi Jinping elaborates it as a "Shared Common Destiny" for mankind, is really only verbiage according to that Kantian outlook.

The Real Kissinger and Allison

In his strange chapter on the "Clash of Civilizations," citing the "genius" of Samuel Huntington, one of the most evil men on the planet, Allison not only lets the geopolitical cat out of the bag; he gives it free rein. He defends Huntington's thesis that, in the current era, new causes for wars are clashes of cultures. There is a very odd characterization of Confucian civilization and an even stranger view of Western civilization, both utterly fraudulent. He emphasizes minor points of difference between Confucian Civilization and Western Civilization, and then concludes with the grotesque claim that the causes for a war of annihilation between China and the West are located in these differences.

As Helga Zepp-La-Rouche has developed in her discussion of Schiller and Confucius, it is, in fact, the *universal characteristics* which define human beings as human, that actually are the basis for escaping the Thucydides Trap.

Yet, ultimately, Allison returns to his basic theme, and insists that the real clash will be the inability of the entrenched power to acquiesce to an ascending power, short of war. For someone like Kissinger, the real point, which is the point that the Athenian Ambassador made to the Melians, is: *"Right is a question which only has meaning for equals."* As Kissinger asserted years ago, in his NSSM 200 memo, the "balance of power" only has meaning for those who have power. For those who don't have power: *reduce their population*. This is the dirty underbelly of Allison's Thucydides Trap.

U.S. Airforce

Caskets of U.S. soldiers being returned to the United States.

Stunning Incompetence or Willful Fraud?

Entirely missing from Allison's analysis is any recognition or discussion of British imperial geopolitics. Every war of 19th Century and the 20th Century was a result of the British geopolitical commitment to maintain their dominance over all emerging powers, beginning with the Russo-Japanese war, manipulated by Britain against Russia, its ostensible geopolitical rival. While Allison's book documents the extraordinary economic take-off of Japan, Germany, and the United States, not once is the question asked: Why this stunning take-off? Allison merely states that fact, yet makes no study as to why that fact is a fact.

In the same vein there is no reason for Kissinger and Allison to complain that America will be eclipsed by China. The Harvard idea that what made America great was "liberal Democracy"—and not the Hamiltonian Public Credit system of production—is incompetent beyond belief. Yet neither Kissinger nor Graham mention the American system even once in their elaboration of the wars of the 19th and 20th Century—the very time period which makes up the substance of the Harvard "Thucydides Study." It is well known that the cause of the eclipsing by Japan of all the Asian powers, was the Meiji Restoration, an event which brought American republican economic methods to Japan. Similarly, Bismarck's Germany began to eclipse Britain after it adopted the American system. Need it be said that we in the United States used our own system to eclipse Britain? So, Japan, Germany, and the United States all eclipsed the dominant, entrenched power, Britain, yet there is not one mention of Hamilton's American System in the entire book.

Allison and Kissinger, in their dry, fact-filled academic recital, deal only with power. They do not distinguish between a system which brings progress to its people and one that brings wars and disaster to its people. Power Is Power. You cannot know Truth, and as a result Justice is also unknowable. The only question for Kissinger and Allison is: How can you keep the conflict below the level of war? There are no universal principles to be studied. You cannot make a moral judgment between different systems. Only the managing of insatiable conflicts, over the long term, is for them the real question.

The LaRouche Factor: A New Paradigm— Escaping the Thucydides Trap

The greatest scientific revolution of the Twentieth Century, arguably, was accomplished by Lyndon La-

Rouche. Henry Kissinger has hated LaRouche for more than forty years, precisely because LaRouche has insisted that morality or Truth, which is another way of saying the Good, can be defined by a scientific standard. Through his work on physical economics, LaRouche has obliterated the idea that the Good is unknowable.

In what can only be described as one of the most stunning forecasts Lyndon LaRouche ever made, he elaborates, in a book chapter, "The Dialogue of Eurasian Civilizations" (in *Earth's Next Fifty Years*), the scientific principles by which mankind can successfully solve what seems to be a set of problems which threaten to destroy mankind as a whole.

LaRouche gets at the core of the issue, with the science of the Good. It is identified by a Dialogue of Civilizations, based on creativity, *per se*. Not rules or formulas, but creative discovery of principles of the universe and the cultures that allow mankind to do that.

The central thesis of LaRouche's book is there are two preconditions for such a dialogue. One is that this dialogue can only be had by sovereign Nation States. The return to such a system breaks the Anglo-Dutch system's hold over the world economic system. LaRouche forecast this in 2004, nine years before the announcement of the Belt and Road Initiative. China, in introducing the Belt and Road, has actually laid the basis for a return to sovereign nation states negotiating their future without that Anglo-American imperial veto. This is most clearly seen today in the return of sovereignty in Africa.

LaRouche's second precondition for such a serious discussion of the Dialogue of Civilizations is that it must focus on the idea of physical economics. LaRouche's discoveries in physical economics are most succinctly defined by the concept of the *Noösphere*, which was developed by Vladimir Vernadsky. Real economics is about expanding mankind's cognitive power in the universe; it is not reduced to money or accounting. It is defined by the relationship of creative discovery by mankind to the biosphere. It is this creative discovery which defines mankind as a unique species. This concept forms the only true basis for a valid Dialogue of Civilizations. Mankind is the most powerful "Geological force" on the planet. Mankind, as a species, increases the rate of free energy for the biosphere as a whole. This impact, identified by LaRouche, is measured by increases in the rate of increase of "Relative Potential Population Density."

In this chapter, LaRouche develops in depth both the nature of creativity *per se* and the concrete actions to be taken to secure the future of mankind as a whole. In the section, "A Fixed Exchange Rate System," LaRouche makes the point clearly:

We must bring to an end the delusion that issues of what is called "culture" could be competently separated from the issue of economy, or that principles of economy might be competently adduced from whatever were chosen as a set of ecumenical cultural values….

The issue of culture is the issue of truth, as the Platonic dialectical method provides a formal standard of truthfulness: not the "absolute truth" of particular ideas of the moment, but the truth of freedom from the effects of reckless disregard for those notions of truthfulness which are best identified with that conception which I have labeled throughout this report as "the living word." By "truthfulness," we should intend to say, "A quality of that which is presently knowable." Even if what is argued were formally correct, without a standard of truthfulness, there is no truth in what is believed, and, as a consequence, society may freely career from one Sophists'-like catastrophe of uncertainty to another. Thus, the idea of truthfulness in policy-making depends upon engaging the populations of each culture in the kind of process I have summarily outlined here. We bring cultures together, by evoking a common experience of living words by means specifically appropriate to the background of shared, or at a minimum, shareable experience.

The object must be, therefore, not a compromise among differing opinions, but a search for the higher truths, …

These brief paragraphs give you a sense of the level of specificity with which LaRouche addresses the question of Truth as the basis for the emergence of the New Paradigm.

The Alcibiades Trap is defined in these new terms of reference. There really is no Thucydides Trap. It is an empty construct, a way of managing the status quo from the standpoint of the British Empire. Mr. Kissinger, Mr. Allison: China will never submit. The rest of the world will never submit. Since there is a fundamental genius on the planet well known by you since 1971, you have no excuse for your new cold war!

Chinese Foreign Minister Outlines 'Major-Power Diplomacy with Chinese Characteristics'

by William Jones, from *EIR*'s European Alert Service

March 10—Speaking March 8 on the sidelines of the National People's Congress, Chinese Foreign Minister Wang Yi gave an indication of China's new policy of major-power diplomacy "with Chinese characteristics." This year's Congress is the first to follow the 19th Party Congress of the Communist Party of China last year, in which President Xi Jinping laid out a broad policy for China in

Xinhua/Li Xin

China Foreign Minister Wang Yi.

this "new era," an era in which China intends to play a greater role in world politics, and to introduce new ideas of governance based on new and old traditions in Chinese culture.

In response to a question on the content of this new style of diplomacy, Foreign Minister Wang said: "In this concept, we will work for the well-being of the Chinese people and the progress of humanity. We will forge a new type of international relations that features mutual respect, fairness, justice and 'win-win' cooperation, and build an open, inclusive, clean, and beautiful world that enjoys lasting peace, universal security and common prosperity." Wang said, "We will stand for equality between all countries, and will oppose the strong oppressing the weak." This was also indicated, he noted, in the development of Xi Jinping's Belt and Road Initiative, which was designed to utilize Chinese economic and technical expertise to help the neighboring countries, and indeed, countries far from China, in Africa and Latin America, in their economic development.

At the same time, Wang Yi emphasized that China was not trying to "replace" the United States as some Western pundits are claiming. He noted that the two countries had "broad interests and a common responsibility" and that cooperation was "the main thrust of the U.S.-China relationship." "If there is any competition between us," Wang said, "it has to be healthy and positive. But competition aside, we don't have to be rivals. The two countries should strive to become partners in cooperation." He emphasized that China's path toward rejuvenation was "unstoppable," "but those who feel that China wants to replace the United States are wrong. China is on its long march toward modernization. It has no need or intention to displace America." China's relationship to Russia was particularly important—"unshakeable as a mountain" is how he put it—and he said that going forward in that relationship, "the sky is the limit."

Wang Yi was particularly emphatic with regard to China's concern for Africa, saying that China and Africa had been "friends in adversity," and that China-Africa friendship was therefore "unbreakable." He also announced that China is prepared to mediate in "flashpoints" on the African continent, and help the African nations in dealing with new unconventional threats such as terrorism. An indication of this concern is the fact that in September, China will be hosting the heads of state of African countries at the Forum on China-Africa Cooperation, as one of the four major diplomatic conferences on China's agenda this year. The three other major diplomatic events hosted by China this year, he announced, will be the Boao Forum for Asia in April, which President Xi will personally address, the meeting of the Shanghai Cooperation Organization in June in Qingdao, and the Shanghai Import Expo in Shanghai in December.

New Connections Enhance Russia-China Trade

by William Jones

March 10—Thoughts of Northeast Asia these days usually involve visions of conflict: the United States vs. North Korea, Japan against China, and Russia against Japan. Nor are these conflicts recent. Manchuria, the northeast province of China, bordering Russia and Korea, is the region from which the conquering Manchus came, the dynasty that ruled China for four hundred years until 1911. And it was here in Manchuria, not in Poland, where World War II actually began when Japan seized it in 1931.

Now the same region is on the verge of becoming a major focus of development and international cooperation under the Belt and Road Initiative. And given the recent thaw in U.S.-DPRK relations, it could become an area of cooperation that also will encompass that "hermit kingdom," the Democratic People's Republic of Korea (DPRK), or North Korea.

The first railroad bridge over the Amur River, which serves as a boundary marker between Russia and China's northeastern Heilongjiang Province, is scheduled to be completed this year. The bridge will connect Nizhneleninskoye in the Jewish Autonomous Oblast of Russia, with Tonjiang in Heilongjiang. The bridge will be 2.2 km long, but its corresponding track infrastructure will be 19.9 km long and is projected to cost $355 million. It is expected to transport more than 3 million metric tons of cargo and 1.5 million passengers per year.

The first railroad bridge was built over the Amur river in 1916, as a part of Russia's Trans-Siberian Railroad. Originally, the eastern portion of the Trans-Siberian Railroad ran not through Russia, but rather through China's Manchuria, stretching all the way to Dalian on the Pacific. A 25-year lease of the right-of-way allowed Russia to build the longest railroad line in the world. It was intended to bring China, as well as Japan, into the major development program planned by Russia's

Xinhua

Railroad bridge nears completion, linking Tongjiang City in northeast China's Heilongjiang Province with Nizhneleninskoye in Russia's Jewish Autonomous Oblast.

Sergei Witte, the Finance Minister who organized the Trans-Siberian Railroad.

The Chinese portion of the Trans-Siberian, called the Chinese Eastern Railway, extended from Chita in Russian Siberia through Harbin, the provincial capital of Manchuria, and then south to Dalian. Another line went west to Suifenhe, near the border, and on to Ussurysk and Vladivostok in Russia. Japanese resistance to this Russian presence led to the Russo-Japanese War and the Japanese occupation of Korea. At a later stage, with the abrupt withdrawal of Soviet advisers from China in 1960, the Amur River became an armed border, with even some military clashes between China and Russia along its length, and virtually no contact across it.

New Economic Corridor

Much of what is being done in the broad context of the Belt and Road Initiative is being worked out in a variety of sub-regional plans. Northeast China's development coordination with Russia's Far East is an example of this. In addition to the direct connections over the Amur River, the China-Mongolia-Russia Economic

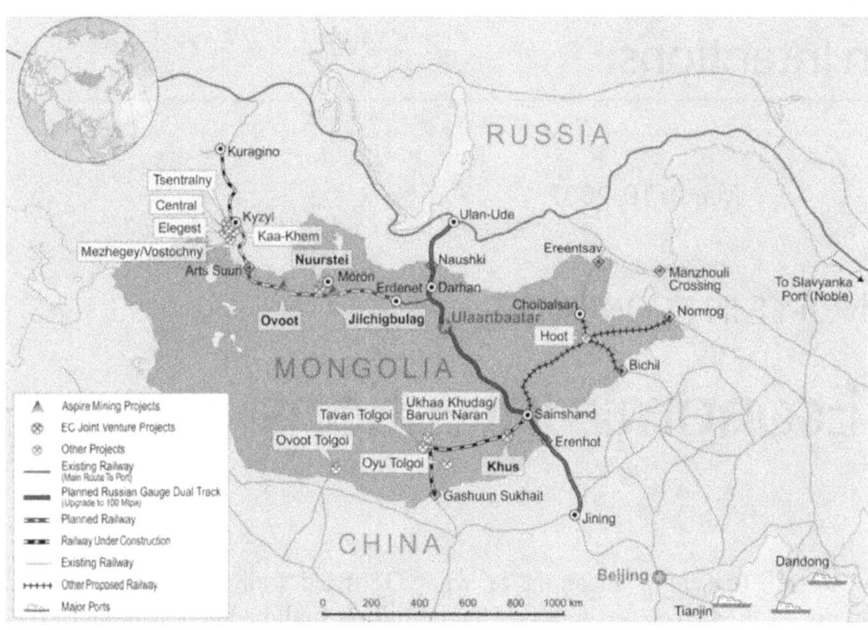

Map of major projects and railway routes joining Mongolia, Russia and China.

border, which has long been the main transit route from northeastern China to the Trans-Siberian Railroad, still carries much of the cargo from northeast China. But already there are nine transit points connecting the borders of Mongolia with China's Mongolian Autonomous Region across the border.

For both countries, this sub-regional aspect of the Belt and Road Initiative is very important. First of all, it facilitates the development of Russia's Far East. Today, most investment in the Russian Far East comes from China. Much of it is investment in oil and natural gas, but with the increasing pace of development, this will significantly branch out into other areas. Before China's "Reform and Opening Up," which began under Deng Xiaoping in 1978, Northeast China was the manufacturing hub of China. But with the development of new industries in the eastern and southern coastal regions as the economy expanded, this area of Manchuria become a rust belt. The Chinese Government is now intent on bringing the economic potential back to this region. Heilongjiang province is also one of the most productive agricultural regions in the country. And if there is peace on the Korean Peninsula, this region will be the key area of confluence with the development of rail connections to North Korea.

Corridor (CMREC) is also being developed. This will make rail connections from Heilongjiang province in China to Russia directly, as well as through the landlocked nation of Mongolia in between them. The leaders of China, Mongolia, and Russia worked out many of these plans at a meeting in 2016. Thirty-two different projects have now been approved for the CMREC, one-third of them dealing with transportation. For the present, trucking remains the primary mode of goods transport, but this will soon change.

An upgrade to the Beijing-to-Moscow rail connection through Ulan Bator in Mongolia is being discussed. The aim of the upgrade is to bring the 7-day trip down to two days, if high-speed rail is used. The Chinese proposal envisions two lines: one, a more direct route from Shenyang in Liaoning province to Chita in Siberia, and a second more easterly line that would connect to the new Tumen high-speed inter-city rail line which goes from Hunchun on the border with North Korea close to Russia, to Jilin City. Many consider the Tumen inter-city line the most scenic high-speed rail line in China. A recent traveler on the Tumen line looked across the river to North Korea, and was amazed how peaceful things looked on the other side. He hardly saw any military installations. Quite remarkable considering the tensions noted elsewhere when speaking of the DPRK.

The port of Manzhouli on the China-Russia

chinadaily

Jilin-Tumen-Hunchun high-speed railway.

March 10, 2001

THE SCIENCE-DRIVER PRINCIPLE IN ECONOMICS

The Gravity of Economic Intentions

by Lyndon H. LaRouche, Jr.

The presently ongoing crash of the world's present financial system, defines a breaking-point in the century of the preceding, post-McKinley-assassination, cultural and political history of our planet as a whole.[1] The fact, that the present financial system is beyond saving, requires our acceptance of the available new system waiting in the wings. In that new system, economic policy is no longer controlled by the financial system, but is coming under the influence of an axiomatic change, in which financial systems become merely useful, and dutiful appendages of a new quality of a global system of national economies, economies modelled upon the precedent of that American System of political-economy, as Hamilton, List, and Carey defined the notion of national economy.

Either the world accepts that proposed, admittedly radical change, and very soon, or, the likely alternative is the plunge of the planet into a spiral of economic and demographic collapse, what is fairly described as a new dark age. Any effort to defend the present financial system, as opposed to the needed, sudden change, will only make the present world economic situation catastrophically worse than if no such rescue operation had been attempted.

Under the needed new system, which must be adopted suddenly and soon, the emphasis will be on physical economy, as I have defined today's applicable meaning of what Gottfried Leibniz named physical economy. That definition shall be the new point of reference for thinking about all matters of both public policy and private economic practice. Money and financial systems will no longer have any self-evident axiomatic authority, but will be subordinated to perform their necessary functions as the disposable tissues of real economy, physical economy.

Most of the elements of that new and far better world society already exist, waiting to be rescued and nourished to strength, once they begin to arise out from amid the rubble of the hopelessly doomed present financial system.

In all really important developments in history, things are never really what traditional ways of thinking have been able to recognize up to that point. The popular mind clings desperately to its old ways of thinking, up to the proverbial last minute, or even beyond that, and attempts, desperately, even hysterically, to interpret the existence of the crisis-elements of a radically changed, new situation, as a continuation of the doomed old, habitual ways.

Yet, recognized or not, the new reality is lurking, waiting to be called on stage, and will rule a new and happier phase in world history, on condition that the threatened dark age is prevented.

If a successful emergence of the new, from the carcass of the old, is to occur, it will emerge as a new form of a society becoming self-conscious of its distinctive nature, its people smiling wryly at the habits of thinking of the virtually illiterate cultural savages they still were at the time the relevant, most recent existential crisis erupted. Those U.S. citizens old enough

---

1. On the significance of the McKinley assassination, see Lyndon H. LaRouche, Jr., on this subject, in, among other locations, "As Seen and Said by the Salton Sea," *EIR*, Feb. 16, 2001, pp. 29-30.

Originally published in EIR, *March 30, 2001.*

Lyndon LaRouche (center) visits a high-energy physics laboratory in Japan, in 1984. The central feature of any effective long-term economic-recovery program for the world today, LaRouche writes, will be a series of "crash" science-driver programs, of accelerated scientific discovery and technological change.

to recall the profound change in generally accepted "values," which occurred as the Roosevelt recovery superseded the Coolidge depression, may recognize the type of social change in values I have just identified.

The developments of the most recent weeks, since the abortive U.S. Presidential election events of November 7, 2000, have changed the world. The things I have been saying for decades, are not merely demonstrated to have been true, but the entry of the world's financial crisis into its present terminal phase, during the recent sixty- odd days, has created a new situation, in which a number of those things which I have stated earlier, and which remain true, must be now, once again, restated, this time in light of the present moments' radically changed world situation. The world is now gripped by a fundamental phase-shift, in which, as is usual for such a situation, things which remain true, must be restated in a qualitatively new context, and, therefore, a correspondingly new way.

Some of those things which need be restated so, include the contents of a recently published book, ***Now, Are You Ready To Learn Economics,*** which contains some crucially important reports on the background to the current situation, which I presented during the

course of the last year.[2] What I have said in those and other locations during the recent months and years, not only remain true, but present events have made them more relevant than ever before. Nonetheless, as you will find in these present pages, last year's concepts must be presented today in a fresh way, as the profoundly more critical immediate situation of the past sixty-odd days demands.

That said, the subject of this report, is a crucial feature of those radical revisions in U.S. financial and economic policies, which are required, not only to overcome the presently accelerating plunge toward a deep world-wide economic depression, but to lay the foundations for the new renaissance of America, in which economics rules over finance, a new type of thinking, which must replace the presently collapsing system. The issue on which I concentrate here, is the unfortunately little understood, but *presently crucial dependency of short-term recovery measures upon an immediate issue of long-term credits for building up basic economic infrastructure and capital-intensive increase of the productive powers of labor.*

Any successful attack upon those problems, whose outcome will determine the future of mankind, must focus clearly upon certain matters of which most economists, journalists, and related policy-influencers are ignorant at this moment. Now, since world events have shown that my long-range forecasts have been consistently correct, and all those of opposing views profoundly misguided, there is a correspondingly increased

---

2. (Washington, D.C.: EIR News Service, Inc., 2000) ***EIR*** has never been produced to be something thrown away, like yesterday's newsweekly; it has been designed to be kept on file, as a living record of the crucial conceptual developments of the decades, since March 1974, when it was founded. My own featured contributions to those pages, during the recent half-dozen years, are of outstanding relevance to the present situation, on that account.

likelihood, that among those who have previously refused to listen, some will now not only pay more careful attention to what I say on these matters, but actually go through the cognitive processes of knowing what I say, rather than displaying a common gossip's Pavlovian conditioned-reflex reactions to, perhaps, the mere mention of my name.

The citizen must now finally face and accept the fact, that the presently ongoing, general collapse of the present world financial and monetary systems, is the product of more than thirty years of widespread professional and popular acceptance of beliefs which are fundamentally contrary to scientific principle. For example, as a matter of principle, Jean-Baptiste Colbert and Alexander Hamilton were right, and Dr. François Quesnay, Bernard de Mandeville, and Adam Smith, typify those perniciously false, but popularized ideas, whose influence on both high places and popular opinion, has misled the world into the present global catastrophe. In these pages, I concentrate attention on that issue of principles first, and turn, in the concluding portion of this report, to the techniques for those principles' application.

The point which I shall bring into focus, in the conclusion of this report, is that, the central feature of any effective long-term economic-recovery program for today, will be the role which *a series of "crash program" types of science-driver programs, of accelerated scientific discovery and technological change,* must contribute, if the world's population is to escape *a long-term economic catastrophe already built into the current state, of combined technological underdevelopment and attrition, of the world at large.*

This poses a profound, and most unsettling intellectual challenge to the present generations of the world's economists and related policy-shapers. The question thus posed is: What intentions must be adopted now, to guide the world's day-to-day policy-shaping in those new directions, which will foster achieving the needed growth in the world's productive powers of labor, ten, twenty, thirty years ahead?[3] What choices of medium- to long-term effects must we project, more or less reliably, from the decisions we make today?

The most important choice, is to know those principles. After that, it is most important to know the

methods by which our nation will be able to forecast those types of reasonably estimated orders of magnitude of medium-term to long-term improvement in per-capita productivity, which may be the best result of the adopted use of those principles. As a necessary, preliminary step, begin here with a review of the role of the calculus in estimating economic progress.

---

1. Actually Knowing the Calculus

The mathematical conception of that problem of economic policy which I have just identified, depends upon competent understanding of the actual nature of Gottfried Leibniz's discovery of the differential and integral calculus, not only in contrast to the pseudo-calculus of Isaac Newton, but also the rejection of that linear perversion of the Leibniz calculus itself, which has been passed down to today's typical modern classrooms, from the hateful work of such fanatical empiricists as Leonhard Euler and Augustin Cauchy.

The crucial point at issue, in defining the calculus to such effect, is the quality of *intention,* which the founder of modern mathematical physics, Johannes Kepler, embodied as the centrally underlying universal physical principle of astrophysics.[4] It is that quality of *intention,* which Euler, Cauchy, et al., removed from the calculus, to produce, thus, their mutilated version of it.

The contemporary economist who has not mastered the rudiments of this issue, is not yet qualified to judge what might, or might not be competent economic-recovery policies for today's situation.

The awful truth to bear in mind, is that the Americas and Europe would not have fallen into the present catastrophe, which has been building up over the recent

---

3. On the subject of "intention," compare Lyndon H. LaRouche, Jr., "The FDR Economic Recovery: Precedent and Practice," Berlin address, March 5, 2001, published in *EIR*, March 16, 2001.

4. It will be made implicitly clear, in the course of this present report, that the effect of the adoption of those "ivory tower" delusions of Aristotle's system which motivated Claudius Ptolemy's hoax, and the impact of both Paolo Sarpi's neo-Ockhamite empiricist dogma and the even more demented practices of the positivists, all have the common effect, of banning the consideration of the causal function of universal physical principles from their systems. Linearization of the Leibniz calculus, as by Euler's dogma, or Cauchy, eliminates the consideration of actual physical cause, *intention,* from the calculations. For example, Galileo made no original discovery, but simply followed the empiricist dogma created by his master, Paolo Sarpi. Thus, the fraud of the modern defense of Galileo from the inquisition, is that Galileo used the same method as the Aristotelean Ptolemy, to reach a conclusion, as an empiricist, which was arbitrarily opposite to that of Ptolemy's dupes, but based on the same violation of truthfulness as that of the Aristotelean defenders of Ptolemy's hoax.

thirty-odd years, had the varieties of doctrines of economics taught in universities not been, chiefly, systemically incompetent ones. Which among them warned of the present crisis, and described its unfolding, consistently, over more than three decades, in precisely the way it has occurred? Which knew what they were doing? Which foresaw the now painfully manifest effects of what they were doing? Let that record of the economy's presently wretched performance be finally heard, speaking for itself.

The explanation of the causes for today's general, systemic failure in the performance of the economists, bankers, and governments generally, must, of necessity, lie in study of those generally accepted beliefs, which were taught in the universities which graduated the relevant professionals. These are the same beliefs also purveyed, as contemporary, credulous popular opinion, by the so-called "Establishment's "customarily lying, mass media. The ideological source of most of the systemic errors, in the teaching of many subjects, is those same sets of axiomatic beliefs, respecting mathematics, which underlie today's commonplace teaching and professional practice in accounting and economics, among many other topics.

The most crippling root-error in the prevalent, contemporary teaching and practice of mathematics, not only among students of economics, but in physical science in general, has been a literally hysterical refusal to acknowledge that basis, in the combined work of Johannes Kepler and Pierre Fermat, most immediately, upon which Gottfried Leibniz's development of the calculus was developed. Had those students taken the opportunity to study the relevant primary sources in the history of modern science, rather than swallowing the generally accepted classroom and textbook gossip, they would have already known the key point I make here.

This lack of this indispensable knowledge, even among many of the most senior physical scientists of today, is chiefly a reflection of pure ideological stubbornness, often veering into hysteria, among the relevant educational institutions and the Babylonian-like peer-review priesthood of the tradecraft's journals. The way in which most university graduates, and others, have been induced to believe the popularly taught errors on this account, is through the cultivation of their fear of that perceived risk to their careers, or simply their reputations among their neighbors and friends, or with the local newspaper editor, if they were overhead saying anything which deviates from what they consider it advantageous to be overheard saying.

Fortunately, the core-problem being addressed at this immediate point in my report, is one within the intellectual reach of any of recent generations of secondary-school students who have been exposed to even a semblance of competent methods of classroom instruction. We focus on that issue of scientific method here, only insofar as that is indispensable for understanding the economic-policy issues immediately at hand. Broader treatment of that scientific question, is left to relevant occasions.

On this account, I encouraged my associate Bruce Director to present an approximately one-hour, video-recorded presentation of the core of Kepler's discovery, as delivered to a recent national conference held in Reston, Virginia.[5] Although this issue had been rather thoroughly addressed, by me and by my collaborators, over earlier decades, to get the same point across to a broader audience, it was pedagogically necessary, given the victimization of recent generations by prevalent, poor standards of contemporary public and higher education, to present the experimental material in the form of animated illustrations, rather than only the otherwise adequate, literary description of the motion to be associated with static images.

A video recording of that approximately one-hour session has been produced. I have proposed that an updated version of that be produced, adding about a quarter-hour, to include a clearer demonstration of that common principle which led to Leibniz's original development of a calculus, and underlay both Kepler's discovery of the principle of universal gravitation, and Fermat's discovery of the concept of a physical principle of "quickest time." I have requested, that an expanded series of such pedagogical exercises be developed and circulated as a much-needed, standard tactic of education in the elementary principles of both physical science and economic policy-shaping.

It is my wish, that the reader should have available a copy of that referenced videotape, either in the form presented at that conference, or the amended version scheduled for later presentation.[6] Here, I limit myself,

---

5. Presidents' Day Conference of the Schiller Institute and International Caucus of Labor Committees (ICLC), Reston, Virginia, Feb. 17-18, 2001.

6. Call 1-703 297-8434 for ordering information.

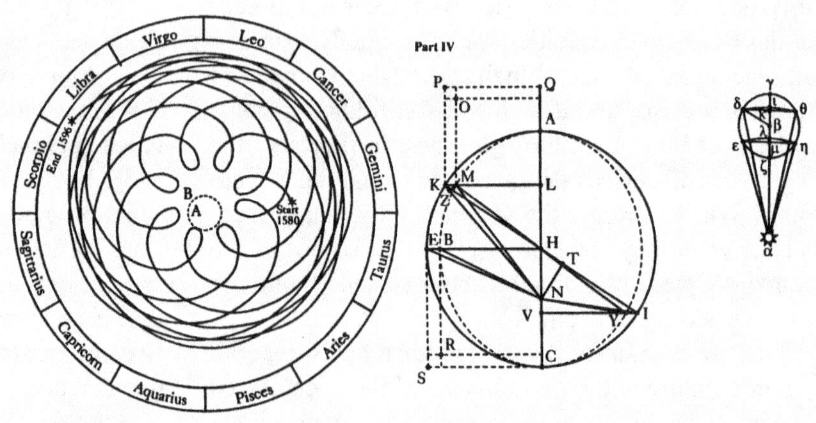

Johannes Kepler, with illustrations from his The New Astronomy. On the left, Kepler's depiction of the "pretzel-like" motions of Mars from 1580 until 1596, as they would have to be drawn, from the unscientific geocentric conception of Ptolemy and Tycho Brahe. On the right, two of Kepler's working diagrams, through which he demonstrated the actual ellipticity of the Martian orbit.

as much as is tolerable, to summarizing those selected, crucial issues of immediate relevance to the subject of economics. To situate the discussion, I summarize the immediately relevant historical background as follows.

Kepler and the Orbit of Mars

The scientific knowledge, that the Earth orbits the Sun, was already well established knowledge within Plato's Academy, prior to the ideologically motivated hoax crafted by the Roman Empire's Claudius Ptolemy. Blind faith in the so-called Ptolemaic system, persisted even in modern European civilization, as recently as the Seventeenth Century, willfully misrepresenting Earth as a fixed point in the universe. This Ptolemaic doctrine was a purely ideological concoction, introduced to bring the teaching of astronomy into conformity with Aristotle. The characteristic feature of that hoax by Ptolemy, is the assumption that science must be limited to abstract deductive concoctions, such as formal mathematical schemes, with no effort to discover the physical causes for action in the universe.[7] That same error has been continued, in an even more vicious version,

and pervasively, by the modern empiricists and logical positivists.

In modern times, the evidence that the Earth moves with respect to the Sun, had been shown by the Fifteenth-Century founder of modern experimental science, Cardinal Nicholas of Cusa.[8] It was a follower of the work of Cusa and Leonardo da Vinci, Johannes Kepler, who settled the issues scientifically, with his original discovery of a principle of universal gravitation, as detailed in his *New Astronomy,*[9] and also the general law for configuration of the Solar System, in his *The Harmony of the World.*[10] Kepler's crucial accomplishment in this matter, was his empirical demonstration of the incompetence of the statistical method employed for mapping observations of the orbits, by Ptolemy, Copernicus, and Tycho Brahe.

The proof of Copernicus' and Brahe's error, subsumed Kepler's discovery of both a universal principle of gravitation, and also, the related harmonic composition of the Solar System's planetary orbits. The relevance of this to a physical science of economics, is that which I have underlined in a previous publication.[11] As

---

7. Modern empiricism, such as that of Galileo, Hobbes, and Newton, is Ockham follower Paolo Sarpi's vulgarization of Aristotelean method; logical positivism, is simply empiricism vulgarized in the extreme. Notably, the exact same "ivory tower" foolishness of the Aristoteleans and empiricists, underlies the argument of the followers of Thomas Hobbes, John Locke, François Quesnay (*laissez-faire*), the pro-satanic Bernard de Mandeville, and Adam Smith, in social theory and economics.

8. E.g., *De Docta Ignorantia.*
9. Johannes Kepler, *New Astronomy* (1609), William Donahue, trans. (Cambridge: Cambridge University Press, 1992).
10. *The Harmony of the World*, E.J. Eiton, A.M. Duncan, and J.V. Field, trans. (The American Philosophical Society: 1997).
11. Lyndon H. LaRouche, Jr., "A Philosophy for Victory: Can We Change the Universe?" *EIR*, March 2, 2001.

I stressed in that earlier publication, as in my Berlin Address of March 5th, the common feature of the physical sciences of astronomy and economics, is the principle of *intention.*

Kepler's solution for defining an elliptical, or approximately elliptical, orbital pathway of Mars (and other planets), was, in first approximation, his adducing the controlling feature determining the combined position and change of velocity of such a non-uniform curvature, according to equality of the area of the angle swept from the relevant focus of the ellipse. That ratio implies the integral value of the orbit as a whole. By adducing the musical-harmonic values of the orbit so defined, and comparing those values for the principal planets considered, Kepler also defined the planetary system, including the specification of a required former planet occupying a harmonic position later shown to correspond to the mass of planetary fragments known, since the work of Gauss, as the asteroid belt.

Thus, in first approximation, the combination of the equal-areas principle respecting each planet, and the harmonic characteristics among those orbits, defined a controlling intention of both the planet individually, and the relative pathways of each orbit within the system as a whole. This combination of conditions which the planetary orbit must satisfy, to reach the next position in a pathway of non-uniform curvature, represented the *intention* which controls such an orbit, as a regular mathematical trajectory could not, prior to Kepler's work.

Such controlling intentions are also called *universal physical principles.* The planet acts as if it were governed by a conscious intention to satisfy those conditions; that intention is otherwise to be recognized as an efficient principle, which acts constantly upon the entire domain in which the action is occurring. That is the simplest of the truthful definitions of a universal physical principle.

From these considerations, Kepler adduced his discovery of a such a principle, known as *universal gravitation,* including what are mistakenly identified by empiricists as "Kepler's three laws."[12] Kepler's relative

success on these accounts, implied the need to supersede what were then generally taught ideas about mathematics, by a new kind of mathematics, one suited for dealing with those physical processes which, like the Solar System, could only be described mathematically as pathways of action with non-uniform curvature. Kepler's relegation of the task of addressing that problem to "future mathematicians," prompted the discovery and initial development of the calculus by Gottfried Leibniz.

This Leibniz calculus employed the concept of the smallest interval of action, as *not* reducible to a straight-line pathway between dots, but a trajectory of categorically non-uniform curvature.[13] It is that view of the calculus, as situated within the context of the Leibniz monadology, which was lost to most modern classrooms, lost through the intervention of empiricists working in the vein of Euler, Lagrange, Cauchy, Clausius, Grassmann, et al.[14] It is the quality of intention, as Kepler defines the notion, which distinguishes Leibniz's related notions of a principle of least action and a monadology, from the reductionist fantasies of an Aristotle, or the empiricists and positivists.

The significance of the Leibniz calculus were better appreciated, when we consider how much the progress of modern experimental science owes to the application of intense rigor to the treatment of what are *relatively tiny, but also globally significant, measurably characteristic differences in long-range effects.* This is the *universally characteristic* feature of the work leading to the founding of modern astrophysics, and the discovery of universal gravitation by Kepler. This, as I shall emphasize in this report, is the key to forecasting the long-range effects of current economic policy.

This focus of experimental method, on seemingly tiny, but persistent margins of deviation from the predictions of some preexisting standard theory, is the history of the development of the notion of the relativity of physical time, from the discovery of a principle of "quickest time," by Fermat, through the development of this notion through the combined work of Huyghens, Leibniz, and Bernoulli. Similarly, we have the case of the proof of the folly of Isaac Newton's doctrine on

---

12. The attempt to reduce Kepler's discovery of universal gravitation, as by the followers of Newton, to the so-called "Three Laws," must be recognized for what it is. In order to detour around the crucial issue posed by non-uniform orbital curvatures, the attempt was made to represent the notion of a universal physical principle as an empirically manifest *intention.* To that latter purpose, the effect of intention was described, by a true believer in the reductionist schemes of Aristotle and

Galileo's master Paolo Sarpi. It is that fraudulent description which is responsible for the three-body paradox of Newton et al.

13. Thus, explicitly contrary to the argument against the monadology by Leonhard Euler, and contrary to the vulgarization of the Leibniz calculus by Augustin Cauchy.

14. LaRouche, op. cit.

'Experts Aghast!'   31

Fermat's Principle of Least Time

When a ray of light passes from air into water, the light ray is bent. In the illustration, AB is the light ray in air, BC, the new direction of the ray after it enters the water. When the ray passes from a less dense to a more dense medium, it always bends towards the normal (perpendicular) to the surface, but the angle depends upon the density of the medium it is entering.

In 1661, a French philosopher and mathematician, Pierre de Fermat, proved that the light bends at such an angle that it always traverses the path from A to C in the least time. This is Fermat's celebrated *Principle of Least Time,* which he hypothesized to be a universal law of nature ("Nature always acts by the shortest course.")

The following consideration might aid in understanding it. Suppose a lifeguard, standing at A, must rescue a drowning swimmer at C. What is his fastest path? As he can run faster than he can swim, to run directly to the water at D, and swim to C would maximize the time spent in the water; it would thus be the slowest path. However, to run all the way to E, and then plunge into the water, while giving him the shortest path through water, would not minimize his time. The path of least time, is to run to an intermediate point B, and then swim a slightly diagonal course

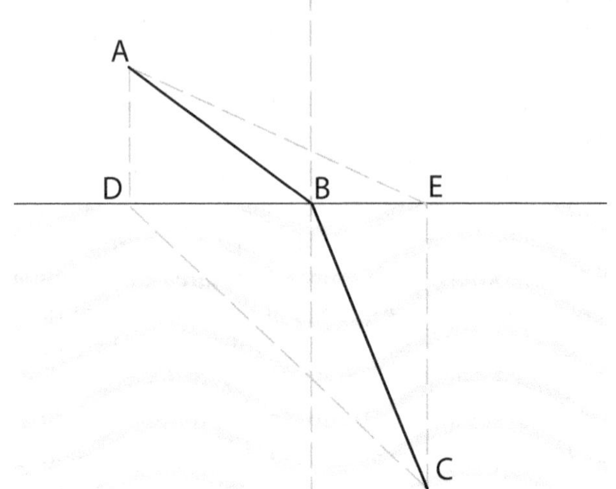

to C. To calculate where the precise point B lies, which will minimize his time, might require a course in optics followed by some calculations, which we hope the lifeguard does not pause to carry out.

Now, consider the light beam, aimed at the point A. When it enters into the water, it will bend at precisely the correct angle, such that, when it reaches C, its total path from A to C will have been completed in the least time. How could the light ray "know" to do that? If Fermat's principle is correct, it is *as if he were attributing a will* to the light ray. So, argued the opponents of Fermat, including the prominent Cartesian, Clerselier, who concluded on this basis that Fermat's Principle must be wrong. But it is not! In this way Fermat's Principle elegantly illustrates the concept of *intent* in nature.—*Laurence Hecht*

light, as Arago's experimental apparatus proved the case for Fresnel's argument.

In partial, first approximation, Kepler's measured trajectory of the Mars orbit, defines the intention of that planet's motion, by the notion that equal areas are swept, in equal time, by the radius of one of the two focii of the ellipse. In Leibniz's hands, that expressed intention of the orbit assumes the form of the non-linear differential of the Leibniz calculus, the form of *nonuniform curvature.* To locate the orbits among the planets, one must refine the differential, in accord with the tuning of the orbital harmonics. Thus, the case of Kepler's determination of the existence of a missing orbit of a planet, later discovered to be the asteroid belt, which must have formerly existed, is crucial experimental physical proof of the validity of both the Kepler conception as a whole, and also the implications which Leibniz adduced for mathematics from Kepler's challenge to "future mathematicians."

In the same vein, the successive contributions to the mathematics of a multiply-connected manifold, by Carl Gauss and Bernard Riemann, provide us today the needed framework of conceptual reference to deal with the evidence showing that life is itself a universal physical principle, existing independently of principles adduced from only non-living processes. Finally, in this same vein, my own original work, in the science of physical economy, enables us today to subsume the notion of a noösphere, as that was defined by Vladimir Vernadsky, within a generalized macroeconomic conception.[15]

These immediately preceding observations bring us to defining the physical significance of a notion of intention, as Kepler employs that for his principal discoveries in astrophysics (and also other cases), and as I emphasize the same notion, as key for long-range forecasting, in the science of physical economy.

The significance of very small margins of difference, is shown most dramatically, by the argument of Vernadsky for the biosphere. The development of the atmosphere, oceans, and so on, by the action of life, over billions of years, corresponds to a major change in the non-living planet, through the cumulative, marginally small, momentary action of life as a universal physical principle. To make clear the significance of the term "universal physical principle," as the empirical evidence of biogeochemistry attests, we must recognize that life, as a category of universal physical principle, is characterized by its expression of an intention which we recognize as making the difference between living and non-living forms of organization.

The actions of human cognition, over millions of years, resulting in the emergence of major changes in the biosphere, include the development of the biosphere to a degree not possible without the cumulative, momentarily tiny, but nonetheless efficient effects of cognitive action. The principle of cognition, like the categorical principle of life, similarly, expressed an intention, an intention which is otherwise identified by a strict use of the term reason.

In each of the three key instances referenced, Kepler's discovery of universal gravitation, and Vernadsky's definitions of the biosphere and of the noösphere,

"My own original work, in the science of physical economy, enables us today to subsume the notion of a noösphere, as that was defined by Vladimir Vernadsky, within a generalized macroeconomic conception."

we have often a relatively very small margin of deviation from what would otherwise be defined as mathematically uniform curvature. This difference is identified by Kepler as corresponding to a margin of *intention,* intention in the sense of action directed by a cognitive mind. In the practice of physical science, experimental physical science as distinct from mere mathematics, such demonstrated cases of *intention* always identify the proof on which the discovery of some universal physical principle depends. The term *intention,* so employed in the sense of Kepler's argument, is equivalent to all proper use of the term *universal physical principle.*

With Bernhard Riemann's 1854 habilitation dissertation, all arbitrary definitions, axioms, and postulates of a formal mathematics, such as customary classroom teaching of Euclidean geometry, are banned from science.[16] They are replaced only by experimentally validated universal physical principles. Each such principle, expressed as an efficient intention, corresponds to a "dimension" of a Riemannian multiply-connected manifold.

In Vernadsky's noösphere, as in the Platonic universe known to the experimental work of Kepler, there are three multiply-connected categories of universal physical principle: a.) non-living; b.) living (biosphere); and, c.) cognitive (noëtic). All three, taken together, are multiply-connected, in Riemann's usage of that notion; all three are equally existent "from the beginning" of the universe so defined.[17] The three, combined as a Riemannian-style multiply-connected manifold, represent a noösphere. My contribution to this configuration, is defining the composition of the sub-manifold of universal cognitive principles. That latter sub-manifold constitutes a category of universal physical principles, so

---

15. It was from the standpoint of this view of living processes, that I developed my original discoveries in the science of physical economy, during the course of work of the 1948-1952 interval. The explicit adoption of Vernadsky's conception of the noösphere, occurred first in my letter of March 1973, leading to the subsequent founding of the Fusion Energy Foundation. See LaRouche, op. cit.

16. LaRouche, op. cit.

17. This is not to argue that human consciousness existed as if "from the beginning," but only that the principle expressed for us as cognition, did.

defined experimentally because its efficient existence is expressed as physical effects which are *intentionally* products of its action. The noösphere subsumed by cognitive action, is the experimental domain corresponding, as subject, to the science of physical economy.

To complete the outline of the point made, concerning scientific method, thus far, I must restate the argument, respecting this use of *intention,* made in an earlier location.

When we today, following Kepler, use the term *intention* as a synonym for the concept of the Leibniz calculus, we are using *intention* as synonymous with *Mind.* Does a planet, then, have a "mind"? Or, is "mind" a metaphor for what Kepler reads as a controlling intention embedded into the planetary orbit by the Creator of the universe? Why should that metaphor be considered as necessary?

In Kepler's work, *Mind* and *intention* are qualities which the cognitive powers of the human mind are able to recognize, as what we may rightly term *universal physical principles.* Man recognizes that distinct quality of Mind, and that corresponding *intention,* as underlying certain distinctive qualities of trajectories. The scientist employs such use of the terms *Mind, intention,* and *universal physical principles,* as of the same set of metaphorical notions, because *the cognitive power of the human is able to recognize the Mind and intention expressed by a Keplerian orbit, as the intention of a universal Being of a nature It shares with the individual human cognitive personality.* That image, of the Creator as made in the cognitive image of man, is the mirror-reflection, for the scientist, of man as developed by the universe, uniquely, in the image of the Creator, that according to the intention of that Creator.

This use of *metaphor* in physical science so-called, is not literary decoration, not optional usage. As I have made the elaborated argument in sundry locations published earlier, any physical principle occurs only in a form which is *not directly representable* in terms of sense-perception.

To represent a principle, using languages which are commonly employed for reporting sense-perceptual types of imageries, we are obliged to resort to ironical juxtapositions of terms, phrases, and clauses, in a language otherwise used for pedestrian sorts of communications. This objective is accomplished in the only way possible, by forcing the mind to recognize a paradoxical expression, which is not explicable in simply sense-perceptual terms. These paradoxical expressions are identified in scholarly usage, as forms of irony, of which the most perfect type is *metaphor.*

In physical science, as usually considered to be distinct from Classical forms of artistic composition, these paradoxes occur in exactly the type of form confronted by Kepler in the matter of the non-uniformity of the curvature of the Mars orbit, and by Fermat in the instance of "quickest time" in refraction of light. The hypothetical intuition of a solution for such a paradox, if that hypothesis is validated experimentally, becomes an addition to the repertoire of known universal physical principles. This discovery of principle then exists as an *efficient idea.* This idea, is not reducible to a form in sense-perception, but rather exists as the unseen object which causes what Plato describes, allegorically, as the perceptible shadows cast on the irregular surface of the wall of a dimly firelit cave.[18]

The recognition of such an experimentally rooted paradox, is an act of cognition, of *Mind.* The paradox, if experimentally validated, corresponds to an efficient *intention,* whose efficiency as a principle exists externally to any object of sense-perception, but whose efficiency as a principle, as an intention, is experimentally demonstrable. Such notions, such as experimentally validated universal physical principles, are ideas in the strictest sense of the term; they exist as objects of thought only within the domain of cognition, but they are rooted in the paradoxes of sense-perception, and are demonstrated to be efficiently existing principles of physical action by their experimentally demonstrable, crucial quality of effects upon the domain of sense-perception.

That connection, once shown, is a subject in its own right; but, one qualification must be made here, and at this point in my account.

As typified by the discoveries which Kepler elaborates in his ***New Astronomy*** and ***Harmony of the World,*** and as Riemann's 1854 habilitation dissertation implicitly defines this notion, the discovery of an experimentally validatable universal physical principle, corresponds to a paradox within the preestablished representation of the universe.[19] Relative to a formal mathematical physics, this paradox is always expressed in terms of what Leibniz named *Analysis Situs,* or paradoxical geometries of position.[20] The first-approximation determination of the Mars orbit, in terms of inten-

---

18. Plato, ***The Republic,*** Book 6.
19. LaRouche, op. cit.
20. Ibid.

tion expressed as equal areas in equal time, by Kepler, typifies this, and, as Fermat's experimental case for a principle of quickest time, also expresses this.

In such matters, the use of *Mind* and *intention* in respect to physical principles, thus signifies the question: "To whose Mind are we referring?"

In the general case, of the universe as merely observed by man, "Who?" is the Creator. In the case of man's efficient intervention into the order of the universe, "Who?" signifies man acting, by nature, as a creature made in the image of the Creator, who, like the Creator, and subject to the limitations the Creator has imposed, acts to impose the intervention of the qualities of Mind and intention into the consequences of mankind's willful interventions.

It is there, and nowhere else, that the subject of a science of economics is situated.

2. Long-Term Investment

There are two currently popular delusions, respecting economies, without which the presently onrushing form of global financial collapse would not have occurred. The name for one of these delusions is "money," as in "monetarism." The name for the other is "the market." Once the student is liberated from that pair of delusions, the true nature of an economy can begin to be brought into focus.

The rational notion of paper money, found its origins as a constitutional idea, early in the history of the English colonies of North America. This idea was first practiced as a successful use of the issue of paper money by the pre-1688 Commonwealth of Massachusetts. That success was referenced in a crucial proposal by Cotton Mather, and echoed afresh by a follower of Mather, Benjamin Franklin.[21] Nonetheless, although the issue and circulation of paper money, as an expression of public credit, by a government, can be a very beneficial practice, paper money itself remains forever "only paper," as the leaders of the Massachusetts Bay Colony made very clear in issuing such currency. Money is sometimes worth less even than the paper on which it is printed, as we ought to be reminded by events such as Germany's 1923 hyperinflation, and both the 1929-1932 and today's collapsing financial markets.

The happier leaders within the Massachusetts Bay Colony already recognized, during the Seventeenth Century, that we must make a categorical distinction between the issue of money by a nation's government, and the use of the form of money circulated from foreign agencies, such as that of the Seventeenth Century's Stuart monarchy of the Massachusetts colonists' time. That difference lies, essentially, in the fact, that our nation is sovereign (or, should be) in the case of a domestic issue of paper currency, and not in the case of our use of a foreign currency. Otherwise, that said, paper money remains "only paper"; neither it, nor so-called "shareholder value," has any intrinsic economic value. Any contrary opinion about money or shareholder value, is to be recognized as a delusion, and, under the circumstances of the world's present financial crisis, a very dangerous delusion, often even, perhaps, a morally criminal, as much as a painful one.[22]

To understand any economic process, an elementary distinction must be made between the two principal sets of relations which define a real economy, which is to say a *physical economy,* as distinct from a mere money-economy. On the one side, we have mankind's physical relationship to nature, as this is measurable in physical terms, per capita and per square kilometer of "macro-economic" area. In the other aspect of physical economy, there are the sets of social relations within society, which affect, and largely govern the willful evolution of society's practiced relationship to nature, per capita and per square kilometer. In relationship to a purely physical economy, money, paper or otherwise, comes into play, as a sometimes useful, as a necessary *political fiction,* in the physical organizing of the social relations within the economy. Paper money, issued as public credit, by a sovereign (or, worse, anyone else), remains always a mere political fiction.[23]

To understand all of those crucial issues of policy-making posed by the present global financial collapse, the most efficient approach is to look at Vernadsky's view of the physical universe as I look at the work of Vernadsky.[24]

---

21. H. Graham Lowry, *How The Nation Was Won: America's Untold Story* (Washington, D.C.: Executive Intelligence Review, 1988).

22. Typical of such delusions is the argument that there exists a category of "honest money," as an alternative to paper money.

23. A monetarist is like the man who took only the shadow cast by his bridge on his honeymoon, while leaving the bride herself, for the rest of eternity, gathering dust at the altar.

24. This also means, to look at the distinction between living and non-living processes as Kepler did, and as Kepler relied on the work of Plato before him. We must include the view of man, as distinct from other

Contrary to the views of the fascist economist Milton Friedman, paper money remains "only paper"; neither it, nor so-called "shareholder value," has any intrinsic economic value.

The first step toward understanding how a real economy works, therefore, is to sort out those connections. All taken together, any economy is essentially a physical economy, and is an expression of a complex of *intentions,* as I have just previously described the use of the term "intentions" in the preceding pages.

On the matter of what might be called a "theory of money," we must, as I shall indicate, derive the function to be assigned to money in a rational way. That is to say, that, in a sane society, it is the physical economy which defines the meaning and value of money; this is in opposition to those foolish people who attempt to derive economic processes as a secretion from one of those "ivory tower" concoctions called "monetary theory."

However, before coming to the matter of the real economy, we must dispense with the second of the two distracting delusions which I referenced above, the delusion called "the market." I shall summarize the relevant argument by, first, quoting once again, as on some earlier occasions, a relevant passage from Adam Smith's 1759 *Theory of the Moral Sentiments,* and then use that citation as the pivot on which to make, once again, my general observation on the heathen doctrine of "little green men under the floorboards," which is the essence of the laissez-faire argument commonly

used by such ideologues as François Quesnay, Bernard de Mandeville, Adam Smith, and Jeremy Bentham.[25]

That adversary of civilized life, Adam Smith, wrote:

"The administration of the great system of the universe … the care of the universal happiness of all sensible and rational beings, is the business of God and not of man. To man is allotted a much humbler department, but one much more suitable to the weakness of his powers, and to the narrowness of his comprehension; the care of his own happiness, of that of his family, his friends, his country … But though we are … endowed with a very strong desire of those ends, it has been intrusted to the slow and uncertain determinations of our reason to find out the proper means of bringing them about. *Nature has directed us to the greater part of these by original and immediate instincts. Hunger, thirst, the passion which unites the two sexes, the love of pleasure, and the dread of pain, prompt us to apply those means for their own sakes, and without any consideration of their tendency to those beneficent ends which the great Director of nature intended to produce by them.*" (italics added).

Decades prior to Smith's writing those lines, the "mephistopholean" Mandeville had already insisted that evil must not be banned, since, according to his argument, it is by allowing both good and evil to have free play in man's affairs, that good will be ultimately brought about. Mandeville's Faustian sophistry is the

---

living creatures, as Vernadsky did, a view which is implicitly pervasive throughout Kepler's work, as in such locations as Plato's *Timaeus.*

25. As cited in Lyndon H. LaRouche, Jr. and David P. Goldman, *The Ugly Truth about Milton Friedman* (New York: Benjamin Franklin House, 1980), p. 107. Mandeville sets forth his pro-satanic doctrine in his *The Fable of the Bees* (1714); the late Friedrich von Hayek designated Mandeville as the virtual "patron anti-saint" of von Hayek's Mont Pelerin Society; Adam Smith was a lackey of Britain's Lord Shelburne from 1763 on; the British Foreign Office's Bentham, another Shelburne lackey, is the putative founder of the utilitarian current in economics.

model imitated by those, such as his devotees of the Mont Pelerin Society, who condemn, invidiously, as "corrupt," adversaries of the "free market" principle, such as governments or persons who oppose legalizing the trade in so-called "recreational" drugs.[26]

Pro-feudalist Quesnay argued that the profit of the aristocrat's estate, was brought into being as a predicate of the aristocrat's mere hereditary title to the estate (e.g., "shareholder value"), on which the role of the serfs was defined, by Quesnay, as essentially that of human cattle.[27] The doctrine of English and British empiricism, introduced to the English-speaking world by Venice's Mephisto-like Paolo Sarpi, defines social processes, including economic processes, as like percussive interactions among Hobbesian particles floating in Euclidean space-time; empiricism defines history, including economy, as a kind of statistical result of those amassed kinematic interactions.

Hence we have in today's U.S., the frankly corrupt doctrine of the "free market" upheld by the Mont Pelerin Society, the American Enterprise Institute, and like-spirited followers of Britain's nastiest nanny, Margaret Thatcher. It is truly a lunatic doctrine, as also a modern parody of the medieval bogomil cult of "the chosen ones."

On the one side, the economists of that curious persuasion insist, that mankind must not interfere with the magical statistical processes of the so-called "free market." At the same time, those brainwashed doctrinaires insist, that that perfectly anarchical market, like a crooked gambling table, is mysteriously rigged, as if by an invisible hand, to ensure that the prices will ulti-

mately be "right," and that privileged people will be rewarded by the influence of some magical taint of bias, a bias in favor of the "chosen ones," built into that crooked gambling-table which that market is in fact.[28]

Neither Mandeville, Smith, nor Bentham, ever claimed to have rational knowledge of why this allegedly perfectly democratic statistical process assured such a statistically consistent, corrupt result. As Smith spoke for himself, blind faith in the "free market" principle, *"prompt[s] us to apply those means for their own sakes, and without any consideration of their tendency to those beneficent ends which the great Director of nature intended to produce by them."* Although they admit they have no knowledge of what the efficient principle is, or how it operates, they insist that it would be morally wrong of anyone, to attempt to interfere with the unfathomable logic of that wonderful underworld domain where such little green men, often disguised as investment bankers, dwell and reign.

If society legalizes crime, it adds criminal proceeds to its official gross national product accounts; if it counts the proceeds of crime as part of the nation's wealth, it thus legalizes crime. If the state intervenes to legalize the international traffic in recreational drugs, the state becomes a drug-pusher, as Secretary of State and H.G. Wells devotee Madeleine Albright's reign did; if it accounts the income of prostitution as part of the taxable gross national product, the President becomes a pimp. In short, leave it up to whatever little green men, whoever or whatever they might be, controlling the universe from under the floorboards of the universal gambling hall. Smith's economics is not science, it is a religion of heathen crap-shooters, probably a tradition of the Babylonian or kindred origins which economist J.M. Keynes attributed to the content of the chest of collected scientific papers of Sir Isaac Newton.[29]

The most insane variety of that English-speaking empiricist tradition, are those monetarist models concocted in the spirit of John Law, in his time, or, in ours, such as John von Neumann's and Oskar Morgenstern's

---

26. This has been the argument in favor of legalization of the cocaine and heroin traffic by such devotees of the Mont Pelerin cult as Professor Milton Friedman. See LaRouche and Goldman, op. cit., pp. 305-322.

27. To situate the role of the strange Dr. Quesnay in the history of political-economy, it is essential to locate the opposition to the policies of France's nation-builders, Cardinal Mazarin and Jean-Baptiste Colbert, by the alliance of the feudalist *Fronde* with that pagan monster Louis XIV. This alliance overlapped the Europe-wide network of salons, operating under the direction of Venice's Abbé Antonio Conti. From the relatively momentary period of a few years, that the possibility existed, that Gottfried Leibniz might become the future Prime Minister for the British monarchy, Conti played the leading role, until his 1749 death, in organizing both the Newton myth, and the anti-Colbert and anti-Leibniz campaign throughout Europe. The position of the disgusting mere tinkler Rameau, and the use of the Rameau myth against Johann Sebastian Bach, were, like the creation of the figure of Voltaire and the role of Quesnay, expressions of the early Eighteenth-century campaigns coordinated by Conti from the Paris of the pagan Sun-King Louis XIV, and of the minority of Louis XV.

28. The type referenced here as "the chosen ones" suggest the cases of two U.S. Presidents Bush, neither of which showed my talent for actually earning money by their own independent skills, but had wealth bestowed upon them by the relevant little green men under the floorboards. See Anton Chaitkin and Webster Tarpley, *George Bush: The Unauthorized Biography* (Washington, D.C.: Executive Intelligence Review, 1992).

29. John Maynard Keynes, "Newton the Man," in ***Essays in Biography*** (New York: The Norton Library, 1951).

radically positivist concoction, *The Theory of Games & Economic Behavior.*[30] Von Neumann, like "information theory" hoaxster Norbert Wiener, was a former acolyte of Bertrand Russell, whose work reflects the wildly ivory-tower rantings of Russell's *Principia Mathematica.*[31]

At their least worst, all of those beliefs associated with today's fashionable varieties of monetarist teaching, are derived from the same "ivory tower" fantasizing which Kepler pointed out as the root of the fallacies of the astronomical systems of Ptolemy, Copernicus, and Brahe. Each fantasist of that collection, begins, as von Neumann and Morgenstern did, with a made-up, arbitrary set of assumptions: the logical positivist's equivalent of a set of arbitrarily chosen definitions, axioms, and postulates. That set of assumptions, like some game just made up by mischievous children, then defines what they are willing to take into account as the acknowledged variety of social facts which they select as belonging to their scheme, their whimsically chosen, childish "rules of the game." That scheme becomes, for them, as for Claudius Ptolemy and his modern dupes, the substitute for a "universe," as represented by the specific mathematical fantasy which they construct.

Other evidence, for which no place is provided in the set of definitions, axioms, and postulates of their system, they ignore, as irrelevant to their system. No physical principles, as I have defined physical principles above, are allowed to intervene in their analysis. On this account, they imitate exactly the willful fraud against physical science perpetrated by Claudius Ptolemy and his modern devotees. The devotees of those constructs then insist upon explaining everything they choose to notice in a real economy, according to the ivory tower model they have constructed.

We shall define a completely different, much happier notion of a market, at a later point in this report.

Biosphere and Noösphere

The principle of production is, that, *through the realization of scientific and technological progress, the average member of the human species, is able to improve the longevity and other demographic character-istics of his or her society's entire population, and to increase its per-capita useful output within a diminishing amount of required, average land-area per capita.* The performance of an economy, is to be measured as the increased production of people, people who are of increased per-capita power to exist and reign, that within what Vernadsky identifies as the noösphere.

The increase of the physical-economic potential associated with the individual can be defined in two distinct, functional ways. Most simply, it implies the individual's potential *for society* within the bounds of the specific state of development of the society/economy within which the individual is functionally situated. However, we have other significant cases, in which we must assess what the individual would have as the more or less immediate potential to become, were he, with his existing personal capabilities, situated in, for example, a less underdeveloped society/economy. To similar effect, we must sometimes emphasize what a present labor-force, or some part of it, has the potential to become merely by virtue of being situated in more favorable sorts of relevant conditions; as for example, the increased potential for society represented by a trained engineer transferred from crude manual labor, to an occupation consistent with his, or her potential.

Such an increase of power, is to be considered as analogous to a trajectory, in the sense that a specific planetary orbit is *a trajectory of constant, if not uniform change,* a trajectory defined by intention. That signifies a quality of trajectory which is distinguished from what is still, today, an ordinary classroom-mathematical type of trajectory, in that it expresses an *intention,* rather than a mechanically predetermined outcome, such as the latter might be implied by the application of conventional methods of today's financial accounting.

We are not defining the individual as, thus, fixed in quality, or of fixed absolute needs. In the language of Heraclitus and Plato, the trajectory of development of the individual in society, and of the society per individual, is *the trajectory of becoming:* of bringing both the individual and the society continually to a higher state, per capita and per average unit of relevant area.

In first approximation, this distinction connotes Kepler's use of the terms *Mind* and *intention.* It signifies, thus, the validation of *a universal physical principle,* as I have defined the correspondence of intention and universal physical principle, in the preceding section of this report. In the case of economy, such intentions include all the connotations associated with the general

<hr>

30. John von Neumann and Oskar Morgenstern, *Theory of Games and Economic Behavior*, 3rd ed. (Princeton: Princeton University Press, 1953).

31. Alfred N. Whitehead and Bertrand Russell, *Principia Mathematica* (Cambridge: Cambridge University Press, 1994, reprint of 1927 edition).

category of regular non-living and living processes; but, in addition to that, there is also a qualitative change included in the connotation. Man's intentions are *cognitively willful,* in a sense that the *quality of intention* associated with either non-living processes, or lower forms of life, is not.

Thus, physical economy represents a category of universal physical principle, but a principle of a different specific quality than either non-living or living processes otherwise defined.

We come now, to the point where we must state and address the crucial paradox upon whose solution all long-range economic forecasting depends. This paradox presents us, at this stage of the report, with an interim result, which I shall now summarize, and address more adequately at a later point in the report as a whole.

At first, perhaps, the argument which I shall introduce in a paragraph a short space below, will not be an easy one for many readers, at their first reading of it. It is paradoxical, but it is essential that it be made; otherwise some essential facts are overlooked. As all important statements of principle, this must be stated in the form of *Analysis Situs,* and must, therefore, assume the quality of metaphor. It is necessary to pose the issue in such a paradoxical way, that the solution to the paradox can be provoked, and then discovered. The secret of knowledge is never to turn one's back on a well-formulated paradox; to turn away from such a paradox, is to turn away from the possibility of gaining what Socrates' principles would recognize as being actually knowledge.

Besides, you should not balk at being challenged to make a serious mental effort. Making discoveries is *fun!* It is fun in the sense connoted by our mind's hearing Archimedes' shout of "Eureka!" People labor greatly to make discoveries of principle, because, as it was for Archimedes, it is great fun to do so. Such fun is a way of life, a way of practicing being alive. It is the quality of playfulness of the great scientific discoverer, the greatest Classical composers and performers. One does it, because it is good to do it.

Having fun, in the sense of Archimedes' cry of "Eureka!" expresses the joy of doing good, and it therefore is the essence of morality. It is the quality of *agapē* of Plato's Socrates, and of the anti-pharisaical (anti-"single issue") Apostle Paul's *I Corinthians* 13.

Science and great Classical artistic compositions are not entertainments; they are a way of life; all progress in the human condition depends upon individual personalities which have such fun in doing good for mankind. *Fun,* as I have implicitly defined a special meaning for that term here, is that special quality of playfulness which sets the happy human child, and the greatest scientist, a Mozart or a Beethoven, apart from, and above the happy playfulness of the boy's companion, that puppy. Thus, I rarely say "Bless you!" to my friends; I deliver a much happier injunction, "Have *fun!*" Or, I enjoin them, "Be careful; don't behave yourself. (Don't be another miserable Kantian!) Have *fun!*" Or, in the terms of Friedrich Schiller, reach upward, from the tragic to the *sublime.*[32]

The result of making such a necessary distinction as I have made here so far, between a universe which includes mankind, and another, which, at least conjecturally, might not, is to imply that the universe in which the universal physical principle known as economy exists, is of the general form of a Riemannian manifold. That universe incorporates three categories of universal physical principle: non-living, living, and cognitive. These specific categories of principles, are multiply-connected, in Riemann's sense. The characteristic of the manifold, is the universal physical principle of physical economy. Such is the nature of the universe in which the sheer fun of human cognition is the dominant consideration, the end-result toward which all multiply-connected features are rightly aimed.

Therefore, now, let us have some *fun!* Start a run of such fun, by noting, that, from this point on, you will be considering a physical economy in its role as a *macro-economic noösphere.* In other words, we are defining the noösphere as "under the management of" a macro-economy defined in the language, and by the methods of physical economy. That means, that we are restating everything Vernadsky has stated for the noösphere and its subsumed biosphere, but, this time, restated, and amplified in the language of my approach to the science of physical economy.

From this standpoint, the functional relationship of the noösphere to the biosphere, is expressed chiefly as

---

32. Friedrich Schiller, "On the Sublime," in *Friedrich Schiller, Poet of Freedom,* Vol. III, 1990, Schiller Institute, Washington, D.C., p. 255. The sublime is the point of difference between Plato and the Classical Greek tragedians, as Plato's Socratic dialogues epitomize that distinction. In modern Classical drama, the notion of the sublime is typified by both Schiller's Joan of Arc and the real-life Jeanne d'Arc whose essential historical reality is captured by Schiller. She died horribly, but not tragically; she spent her life for a mission of great outcome for European civilization as a whole. So, the truly sublime Christ, no tragic figure, died for the benefit of all mankind.

what macroeconomics views as *basic economic infrastructure.* This means, chiefly, *the development of the land-area of a national physical economy as an indivisible unit of action, that over a relatively long-term period of not less than approximately a quarter-century, or even much longer.* This apparently paradoxical principle of national-income accounting, is crucial; therefore, I elaborate the point I have just made.[33]

The most general of the inherent fallacies of today's conventional financial accounting and national-income accounting practice, is of the same type as those who, unlike Kepler, tried to explain astronomical processes in terms of simple mathematical connections among observed point-positions of celestial objects. Just as Kepler recognized the importance of adducing the moment-to-moment principle governing an orbit, from the study of the paradoxes posed by the orbit as a whole, so we must judge the significance of localized, relatively short-term economic developments from the vantage-point of both the whole process within which those developments are situated, and over a time-span sufficiently long to expose the long-term major effects of what seem small, even insignificant variations within a small portion of the short-term developments.

Generally, the minimum interval of time, during which the relationship between short-term aberrations and their large-scale long-term effects, becomes empirically clear, is in the order of not less than a quarter-century, approximately the span of development of a newborn childhood into a fully defined-as-functional adult individual. How, then, can we know results of today's actions, a quarter-century or more hence? How do we know the orbit of the planetary body on which we discover ourselves travelling at this immediate moment?

Since infrastructural development, and long-term capital improvements, or the lack of either or both, define the net outcome of an entire generation of an economy's unfolding, we must never attempt to define

---

33. This is the paragraph of which I forewarned you a bit earlier.

the policies properly governing so-called microeconomical functions, except in an axiomatically well-defined macroeconomical setting.

Why the U.S. Is Bankrupt

Take as an example, the trillions of U.S.- dollars-equivalent of unremedied attrition of basic economic infrastructure since the Nixon Administration. See similar trends in continental western Europe, and the worse state of affairs similarly induced within the United Kingdom, as in the brutish looting and ruin of the economies of New Zealand and Australia. Under existing, post-1965-1972 trends in policies, that damage to those economies could never be reversed, but, in fact, would become ever worse, and inevitably so.

There have been several ways, which, combined in effects, have contributed to the ability of governments and others, to concoct fraudulently optimistic reports on overall national economic performance of these nations' economies.

One way has been to conceal the increased degree of looting of nations outside the U.S.A., western continental Europe, and the so-called "developed" nations of the British Commonwealth, by collusion among the world's London financial center, the IMF and World Bank, in organizing runs on national currencies [**Figure 1**], and against specific commodities. By aid of these measures, national currencies were, repeatedly, arbitrarily depressed, and the foreign indebtedness, including debt to the IMF added, as a way of deflationary looting of the

Increase of Actual New Car Price Compared to BLS Computation of CPI for New Cars

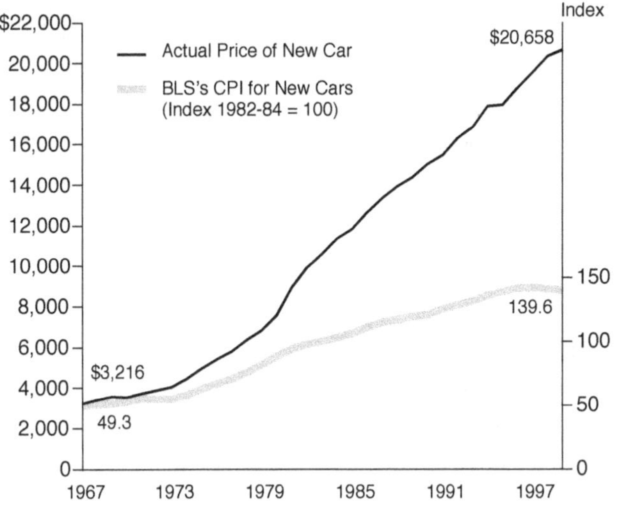

Sources: Department of Commerce's Bureau of Economic Analysis; Department of Labor's Bureau of Labor Statistics; *EIR*.

continents of South and Central America, Africa, and so on, under the so-called "floating exchange-rate" monetary system. This latter was called the "liberal system," because it enabled predator nations to loot victimized nations and continents so liberally. The prosperity of the U.S. and the British monarchy's reign, and also western Europe, such as it has been, has depended increasingly on this specific method for post-1971 looting of the nations of South and Central America, Africa, the former Comecon bloc, Southeast Asia, and so on, under the so-called "floating exchange-rate system."

Another way of perpetrating the fraudulent appearance of net profitability of the predator nations' economies, was to understate the rate of inflation in those economies. One of the most naked of such frauds perpetrated by the U.S. government, was a practice which I denounced in a national TV network broadcast, early in 1984: the hoax called the Quality Adjustment factor [**Figure 2**][34]. That hoax continues to be perpetrated, to the present time.

Another accounting swindle to kindred effect, was simply ignoring the material loss to the national economy from depreciation and depletion of basic economic infrastructure [**Figures 3** and **4**]. By failing to take the current cost of replenishment of this margin of depreciation and depletion into account, in national income and product accounting, the irreversible loss to the future of the economy, caused by abandoning essential infrastructure, was fraudulently suppressed for sake of

---

34. The broadcast was aired on ABC-TV on Feb. 4, 1984, during LaRouche's campaign for the Presidency.

U.S. Railroad Mileage

(Miles per 1,000 Households)

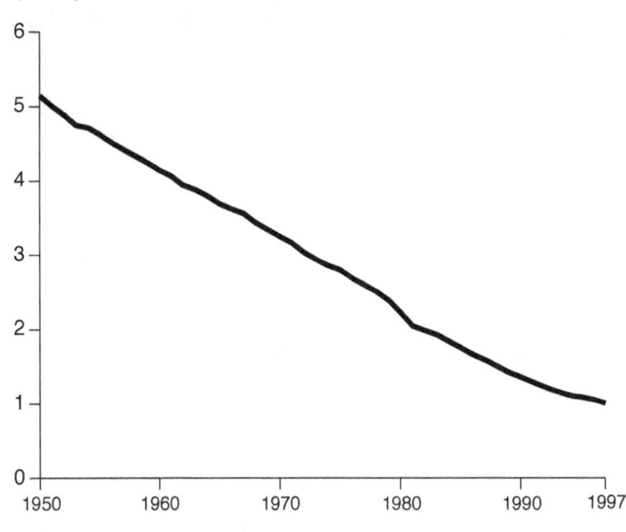

Sources: Association of American Railroads; U.S. Department of Commerce, Bureau of the Census, *Population Surveys*, various years.

Hospital Beds per 1,000 U.S. Population Overall, and in Community Hospitals

(Beds per 1,000 People)

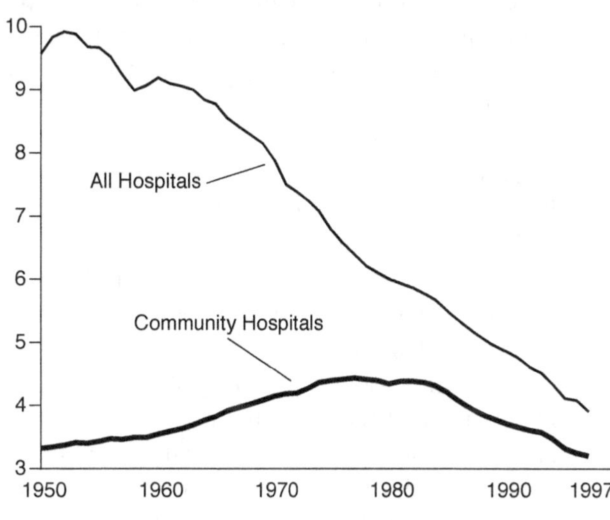

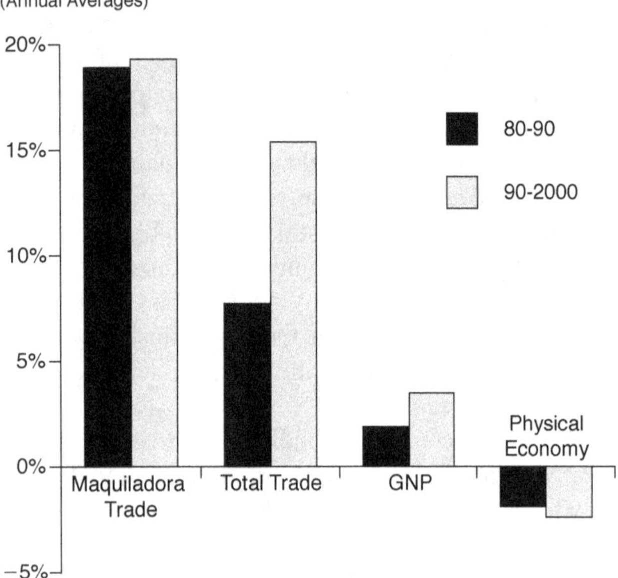

Sources: Banco de México, INEGI; *EIR.*

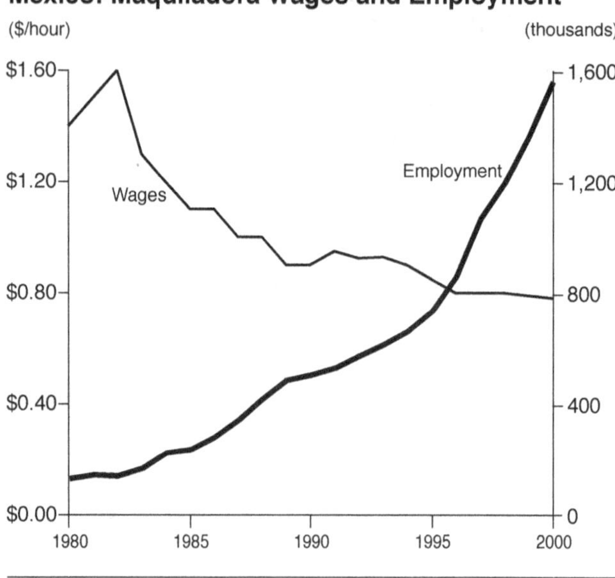

Sources: Banco de México, INEGI, CTM; *Twin Plant News*; AFL-CIO.

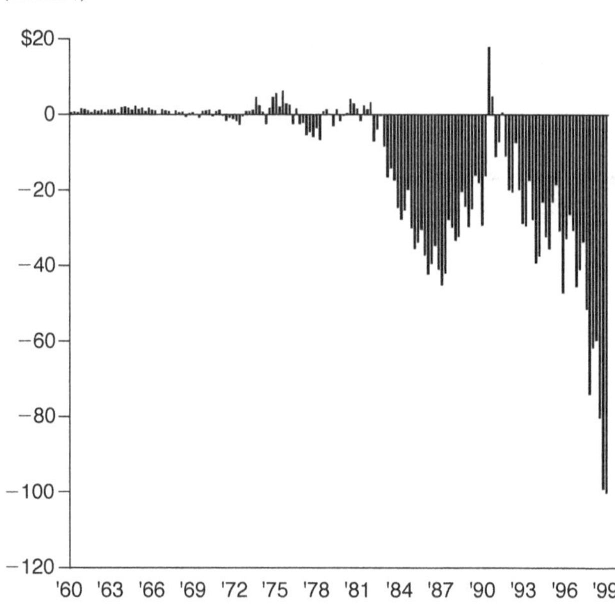

Source: U.S. Department of Commerce.

presenting a success-story, where ruin was actually in progress.

NAFTA and "globalization" generally, have looted most of the world in a two-fold way. The production of more and more of the commodities used in so-called industrialized economies, was "outsourced" to cheap-labor markets abroad [**Figures 5, 6,** and **7**]. The included results, were the accelerated collapse of the earned real income of the U.S., for example, the vanishing of essential production capacities and productive skills from the thus-depleted, importing former agro-industrial powers, and the devastating collapse in the real income-rates of the lower eighty percentile of U.S. family households, for example.

Typical of one of the relevant greatest accounting swindles of them all, was the 1995-2001 hoax called "Y2K." Under the pretext, that a computer-accounting disaster threatened the world economy on Dec. 31, 1999, a vast financial bubble was generated in the area of what was called, variously, "information technology," or the "Third Wave" [**Figure 8**]. While some part of the computer and related technologies involved are intrinsically potentially useful, especially for administrative functions, the "new economy" bundle was, predominantly, a vast swindle, with about the same benefit to national income as might be reflected in IRS esti-

mates, that by legalizing prostitution, legalized supermarket sales of heroin and cocaine, and legalization of all forms of crime generally, the national income might be increased.

Virtually all of those factors on which net rates of sustained real physical-economic growth depend, were buried under an avalanche of bubbling swindles of one variety or another.

Thus, we have come to the point today, that the outstanding financial debt of the world at large, could never be paid by a world economy attempting to meet those presently required, cancerously multiplying demands for payments. The reason we have entered the worst, greatest financial collapse in all human existence, now, is that the reported economic growth of the world's economy, especially of Europe, the British Commonwealth, and the U.S.A., of the past thirty years, has been one gigantic swindle. The cupboard is bare, because it has been emptied, not by ordinary burglars, but by the lunatic, Thatcher-like greed of the London-centered shareholder-proprietors themselves.

By the standard I have specified above, and taking related facts into account, the so-called developed sector of western Europe, the Americas, and the British Commonwealth, has not actually earned a net profit, as national economies, since the tragic trends set into motion over the 1964-1972 period, by that pestilence typified by Wilson in Britain and Nixon and his "Southern Strategy" in the U.S.A. All reports of net growth in national incomes of these nations over the period since, have been a gigantic accounting fraud. It was my recognition of, and understanding of that *systemic* fraud and its nature, which was essential to my becoming the most successful long-range economic forecaster known to the public in the world at large today.

Basic Economic Infrastructure

From the standpoint of Vernadsky's outline, this development of basic economic infrastructure is expressed in two clearly distinguishable ways. In some actions, mankind's action simply improves the development of the biosphere as man finds it, as through the transformation of arid regions into biologically rich farmlands.

In the second class of actions, man improves the variety of content of the biosphere, qualitatively, by adding to it new kinds of what Vernadsky calls "natural objects,"[35] adding to the repertoire of natural objects already produced by forms of life inferior to mankind. Such "natural objects" introduced to the biosphere as products of cognition, include transportation and power systems. Water management systems represent the combined effect of human promotion of the kind of natural objects already produced by the biosphere as such, combined with added elements which are natural objects of a type unique to the products of cognition. Urban development is chiefly an example of natural objects of cognition.

The development of educational systems, like the role of principles of Classical artistic composition, is a part of the essential infrastructure of the biosphere; but that is a matter to be taken up in the more suitable setting of review, conducted in the immediately following section of this report, of physical economy as a social process, rather than as simply the measurable relations as defined, in effect, per capita and per square kilometer.

For reasons which I shall clarify at a suitable later point in this report, it is necessary to make a certain functional distinction between what is usefully designated as basic economic infrastructure, and other qualities of specifically economic activities.

Broadly, the distinction is, that basic economic infrastructure's development and maintenance, reflects a society's conscious sense of its government's unique responsibility for the economic and related potential embodied in the improvement of *the land-area as a whole,* and *the population considered immediately in its entirety.* Thus, these represent the accountability of the government for the promotion of the interest of the cause of the general welfare, as represented, inclusively, by the entirety of the land-area, per se, and the entirety of the population, per se. Thus, basic economic infrastructure is distinguished from that which, under the American System, usually falls within the province of private entrepreneurship, such as agriculture and manufacturing industry. There is, as I shall show in due course, a deeper distinction, but what I have just stated will suffice as a working observation at this juncture.

Usually, areas other than basic economic infrastructure, are associated with the application of man-made discoveries of universal physical principles and their derived technologies, to the design of products and pro-

---

35. "Natural products" is employed here in the sense of Vernadsky's argument. As cited in Lyndon H. LaRouche, Jr., "A Philosophy for Victory: Can We Change the Universe?" *EIR*, March 2, 2001, see footnote 11. Also see Vladimir I. Vernadsky, "On the Fundamental Material-Energetic Difference Between Living and Non-Living Natural Bodies in the Biosphere" (1938), Jonathan Tennenbaum and Rachel Douglas, trans., *21st Century Science & Technology*, Winter 2000-2001.

ductive processes. This is usually associated with an entrepreneurship of one or a number of persons, acting within the bounds of general law for the society as a whole, but on their own initiative.

In general, functionally, the existence of the latter entrepreneurships is situated on the basis provided by the development of the society's basic economic infrastructure. Their potential is delimited by the quality of environment which the development of the basic economic infrastructure represents. In general, an enterprise situated in an area with relatively poor development of basic economic infrastructure, has a lower potential than the same enterprise would represent, if situated in an area of better development and maintenance of basic economic infrastructure. The latter is typified as among the ultimately terrible errors in the recent decades' resort to "outsourcing" and "globalization."

Thus, in modern society, roughly forty to sixty percent of the total investment in development and maintenance of a healthy national economy, will be situated within the domain of basic economic infrastructure. Such development and maintenance of basic economic infrastructure will always be conducted under regulation by the society as a whole, and may be largely, even entirely an economic function of government. This is necessary, since only government has responsibility for, and authority over all of the land-area of the nation. Only the government of a truly sovereign nation-state has the competence to assume responsibility for the assured payment of debt-obligations incurred on the kinds of long-term accounts which the development of basic economic infrastructure incurs.[36]

However, since the development and maintenance of basic economic infrastructure depends largely upon its own consumption of the products of production, both directly and indirectly, the investment in the development and maintenance of basic economic infrastructure, is a principal stimulant for the growth and mainte-

nance of the level of output and productivity of the population and its production as a whole.

In the general form of the functional relationship between the noösphere and biosphere, we are presented with two kinds of expression of qualitative change which the macroeconomic development of the physical economy introduces into the development of the biosphere and noösphere alike. One kind of qualitative change is associated with extension of scale of development, without the additional introduction of new kinds of "natural products" of the noösphere; the other, with the introduction of new qualities of "natural products" of the noösphere.

For example, the simple extension of large-scale water management, extended development of agriculture, and of managed forests, increases the amount and effective energy-flux-density throughput of "biomass" over large areas, with associated qualitative effects on the weather systems within entire regions. Such transformations complement, but are distinct from the transformations caused by introduction of new kinds of natural products of the noösphere to the biosphere. Thus, we must distinguish between qualitative effects of increase of scale and intensity of use of existing programs and technologies, and the qualitative effects of introducing new kinds of technologies, or even new, virtually man-made physical principles of practice.

In the longer run, it is the role of the introduction of new kinds of "natural products" of cognition (discoveries of universal physical principle and their technological derivatives) to become an integral part of the functioning of basic economic infrastructure, which is determining. Despite that, the qualitative improvement in the characteristics of land-area, as biosphere, and as infrastructure, through extended application of already existing principles, is extremely significant.

Functions of Physical Economy

So far, as a matter of emphasis, I have confined the development of my argument to the first aspect of scientific and technological progress: our species' increase of its power over nature, as measured per capita and per square kilometer. I have referenced the cultural factors, but have not integrated their role. For the remainder of this section, I shall continue to maintain that emphasis. That limitation should be taken for granted by the reader, until we come to the following section of the report.

The essential feature of the process by which man-

---

36. On this account, the development of the principle of Chapter XI bankruptcy, during the 1930s, remains indispensable policy for any area of long-term commitment to the development and maintenance of basic economic infrastructure, such as a public-health system for a nation, a region of a nation, a region of the planet, or the world as a whole. The claims of debtors' creditors, in such bankruptcy proceedings, must be subordinated to the public interest, that according to the U.S. Constitutional principle of the general welfare. Thus, government meets its responsibilities for honorable treatment of debt incurred in an honorable way to an honorable purpose. This obviously conflicts with any claims presented on the account of a predatory form of "shareholder interest."

kind increases its species' power to exist, in and over the universe, is the discovery and application of additional, validated discoveries of universal physical principle. In the experimental validation of such a discovered principle, the design of that experiment includes willful features which express the new principle being tested. Those features of a successful such experiment, then become, in turn, the model for applying the validated principle to man's willful control over nature. The class of derivatives of successful such proof-of-principle experiments, is called *technologies.*

These technologies appear in various guises. They appear in a somewhat different form in their application to different kinds of materials. They also appear in the testing and measurement of the functional relationships among varying combinations of materials and technologies.

For example, the fact that a technology works in its direct application to one choice of material, does not mean that it will work in the same way in another. Nor, can we assume that a technology will work to the same effect when a change is made in the combinations of technologies employed for a common function, or when a different material is substituted.

All these and related challenges require the ministrations of a class of specialists expert in the matter of designing the apparatus appropriate to, and conducting proof-of-principle experiments. The attempt to substitute computerized "benchmarking" for such traditional engineering abilities, invites catastrophes. *The universe is not linear.*

With those and related kinds of considerations taken into account, the immediate relationship of human action to the universe, is a function of the accumulation of valid new discoveries of universal physical principle. This includes the categories of universal physical principles specific to living processes, and also to cognitive ones. For the moment, the argument is made only for the case of non-living and living processes, not cognitive relations among persons. With that restriction, man's power in and over the universe, per capita and per square kilometer, is bounded by the accumulation of valid discoveries of universal physical principles.

This signifies, that man's per-capita power in and over the universe, as the universe is defined in terms of mankind's per-capita relationship to it, is to be seen as a function of the accumulation of valid discoveries of universal physical principle. It is the application of that accumulation, in whole, or in part, which delimits man's potential power in the universe.

In that sense, the universe, as defined in terms of mankind's relationship to it, is Riemannian. By Riemannian, I mean, in first approximation, the then-revolutionary implications for mathematical physics, of Riemann's 1854 habilitation dissertation.[37] Each validated *intention,* otherwise known as a *universal physical principle,* functions as a "dimension" of a physical geometry from which all so-called Euclidean and related sets of arbitrary definitions, axioms, and postulates have been excluded.

Such a geometry of "n" such dimensions, differs from a kindred geometry of "n+1" dimensions, by an experimentally defined change in "curvature" in passing from one to the other. In physical economy, this is expressed as a change in the characteristic curvature of an economic action occurring within the system as a whole.

So, to illustrate that point in the relatively simplest terms, the introduction of large-scale application of electrical motive-power for individual machinery, replacing reliance on belt-driven-shaft systems used for entire factories, represented a qualitative change in the characteristics of the actions performed by the relevant operatives of machinery, even when the skills and techniques of the operatives were not changed in other respects.

In first approximation, a Riemannian geometry premised upon that habilitation dissertation, would be presumed to include only one class of universal physical principles. In the case at hand, the noösphere as a physical geometry, we have three distinct, but multiply-connected classes of principles: non-living, life, cognition. There is no inherent objection to treating this case as a Riemannian geometry in the conventional sense of Riemann's own intentions.

To the degree such a Riemannian geometry is embodied efficiently in the macroeconomic noösphere in which the members of a society exist and act, a change from a geometry of designation "n" to one of designation "n+1," signifies an increase of the net power of the average action taken by the individual existing and acting within the framework of a noösphere of that latter designation. In other words, an increase in the

---

37. Bernhard Riemann, *Über die Hypothesen, welche der Geometrie zu Grunde liegen, **Bernhard Riemanns gesammelte mathematische Werke,*** H. Weber, ed. (New York: Dover Publications reprint, 1953).

relative anti-entropy of the system, and also of the action of virtually every person within that society.

Some brief practical illustration of this principled conception is in order at this moment.

When we increase the availability of usable water, of sources of power of increased energy-flux density, of more rapid, more efficient transport of people and goods, we improve the available performance of each person in that society, even if no other change in their behavior is introduced. If we improve both sanitation and health-care, thus reducing the economic losses attributable to illness, impairments, and death, we increase the productivity of that society as a whole.

If, on the other hand, society's zeal to reduce the cost of goods to the lowest possible price, prompts it to cut back on both public expenditure for basic economic infrastructure, and also to eliminate regulation of this area to the effect of ensuring its development, then the average productivity of the labor-force will collapse, as a result of the lack of meeting the costs to be included in prices of all goods, and of developing and maintaining basic economic infrastructure.

3. Physical Economy as a Social Process

In the opening section of this report, on the subject of the Leibniz discovery of the calculus, I distinguished the notion of processes governed by a universal physical principle, as expressed in the form of *intention,* from that false, mechanical notion of "causality" associated with the work of empiricists such as Isaac Newton and his followers. The latter, mechanical notion, is the false, "Newtonian" notion of "causality" which is still widely accepted in the secondary and university mathematics classroom, today.

As I have also stressed there, in physical systems, we are confronted with two general classifications of intention. In the one case, we have the ordinary *intention* expressed in the non-mechanical determination of a result by a universal physical principle, such that expressed by a Solar orbit, or the consistent difference which may be manifest, between what are otherwise ostensibly identical chemical processes, when one is associated with a living process, and the other not. In the other case, we have the notion of *willful intention,* in the case of an original cognitive discovery, or its reenactment by a second person. It is the social implications of

the second type of case, to which this report turns your attention now.

Empiricists, such as empiricist Galileo's mathematics pupil Thomas Hobbes, degraded society into a collection of so-to-speak kinematically interacting individual objects, like the particles of a gas theory. They assumed a set of fixed, built-in definitions, axioms, and postulates, as underlying the possible behavior of these particles. This is the system of John Locke, satanic Bernhard de Mandeville, David Hume, Adam Smith, and utilitarians such as the British Foreign Office's Jeremy Bentham. That is the underlying basis for their definition of what they term "human nature." Empiricist-turned-Aristotelean Immanuel Kant, insisted upon the same underlying notion. The modern logical positivists have carried that notion to extremes, beyond even that of which the depraved old Hobbes might be accused.[38]

Put the point in the following terms. If, as I have shown repeatedly, the distinction between the human being and the beasts, is the power to discover a valid universal physical principle, what is the corresponding, natural expression of human relations? If such a discovery typifies the human individual's characteristic potential, what are "human relations"?

It is the communication of those ideas corresponding to valid universal physical principles, from one mind to another, which enables the human species to behave as a human species, rather than a mere interacting collection of particle-like human individualities. It is the accumulation of the transmission of such discoveries of principle, over successive generations, which distinguishes the human species, as a species, from the beasts which Hobbes and his admirers aspired to become. Thus, how does this communication of such notions of principle occur? How therefore, does mankind develop as mankind?

The pivotal question, so posed, is: How does the transmission of the idea of the actual discovery of a

---

38. Kant makes clear, most emphatically so in his **Critique of Judgment**, that the empiricist principle, which he defends from a quasi-Aristotelean standpoint, is a principle of pure irrationalism. He makes the point most explicitly in respect to aesthetics, in which he shows himself a pure romanticist, in the literally pagan-Roman sense of *vox populi.* The same is true of G.W.F. Hegel's fascistic (i.e., Napoleonic) theory of the state as revolution, as echoed by Carl Schmitt during the Twentieth Century. Similarly, the empiricist, positivist, and existentialist doctrines of "free trade" and "globalization" today, are based upon the pure irrationalism which is axiomatic in the arguments of Hobbes, Locke, Mandeville, Quesnay, Hume, Adam Smith, Bentham, et al. before Kant.

valid universal principle occur? I have covered this in so many previously published locations,[39] that I need only summarize the response, once again, here.

The discovery of an *idea,* a platonic form of idea, as the discovery of any valid universal physical principle typifies this, can not be communicated from one person to another in the medium of sense-perception as such, but only by replicating the act of discovery and validation. This is precisely what does occur in any system of education consistent with Classical humanist principles, such as those of Germany's exemplary, former Humboldt reforms.

The distinction of the human being from mere animals, such as the higher apes, is the ability of the human will to discover the quality of intention which I have associated here with what Kepler called *Mind* or *intention.* By adopting that intention, such as a valid universal physical principle, as our own intention, we are able to exert that idea as an efficient act of the individual human will, as a universal physical principle, upon the universe. The ability to discover, or recognize such a quality of *idea,* depends upon our creating that idea within our own cognitive processes. Typical is such transmission of such platonic forms of ideas from Plato's dialogues to the present-day reader, approximately 2,500 years later. It is sufficient that today's reader relive the drama of the Plato dialogues, thus to find himself, or herself, a living participant today in the dialogue as it occurred then.

To identify the method of such transmission, I describe the process once again, summarily, now.

Ideas come into existence as ontological paradoxes. That is to say, more precisely, ideas come into existence in response to what the conscious mind is able to represent to itself in the form of such a paradox. A well-stated such paradox, is represented in the form known as *Analysis Situs,* or, in Classical artistic composition, as *metaphor.* Given the equivalent of a standard theory, if the experience of an actual event or condition, requires that experience be stated by standard theory in ways which are either simply outside, or represent an impossible inconsistency within that standard theory, the juxtaposition of two or more mutually contradictory statements, each consistent with standard theory for describing events, represents an ontological paradox within the terms of that standard theory.

The paradox of the Mars orbit, as adduced and presented by Kepler, is an example of the way in which a statement in the form of *Analysis Situs* arises within the framework of reference proffered by a prevalent standard theory. If a validated *hypothesis* is discovered, which creates a new standard theory eliminating the ontological paradox, we have the discovery of a new valid universal physical principle.

Thus, we have the three-step method by which valid universal physical principles are made known, and communicated so from one person to another. First, there is the valid statement of an ontological paradox. Second, there is the formation of an *hypothesis,* as a proposed solution for that paradox, in the mind of the individual. Third, there is the demonstration which validates the hypothesis as a universal physical principle.

Although, no such idea can be perceived by sense-perception, the first and third steps so indicated, are rooted in sense-perception. The paradox is demonstrated to be a paradox by the standards of evidence applicable to sense-perception. The validation of the hypothesis is similarly experienced. By aid of those two reference-points, two persons can recognize that they have experienced the same formation of an hypothesis. That validated hypothesis is a Platonic *idea. All valid notions of universal physical principle, of all types, are Platonic ideas,* and, like the ideas of functions within the domain of atomic and nuclear microphysics, could not exist in any different form.

Thus, to enable a student (for example) today, to know what principle Kepler discovered, that student must replicate Kepler's experience in such ways as re-experiencing each step of Kepler's experience, as reported by him in **New Astronomy** and related relevant locations. This method, which is the direct opposite of today's customary textbook education or other transmission of mere "information," is the Socratic method, or, what is otherwise known as a Classical humanist mode of education.

In such ways, persons long dead transmit ideas to us from the past, as if they were alive and speaking directly to us today. Similarly, ideas are transmitted in a cognitive mode among contemporaries, sometimes over great distances. So, we speak to the future.

However, we must go a step further at this juncture. We do not know ideas of that sort in isolation from one another. Knowledge is not only the accumulation of in-

---

39. LaRouche, op. cit.

dividual such ideas; knowledge is a process of integrating an ongoing accumulation of such ideas, into the kind of world-outlook which Riemann's habilitation dissertation implies.

Ideas are produced by the influence of previously extant ideas, in enabling us to define and resolve newly considered paradoxes of an ontological quality. By this process of integrating assimilated, discovered, and rediscovered ideas of universal physical principle, we develop a quality of mind which may be regarded as "hypothesizing in general," as a way of thinking about the universe.[40] So, the process of discovering individual new universal physical principles, and integrating such discoveries of principle with our knowledge of principle in general, becomes a self-developing philosophical world-outlook.

Although two persons who have shared the same experience of an idea, may recognize the commonality of their cognitive experience of the idea's generation, that does not suffice to enable them to recognize that idea as *a distinct idea*. Ideas become distinct for the conscious mind as they are integrated in a process whose implied goal is an unfolding process of hypothesizing-in-general, a process of the form implied by Riemann's habilitation dissertation. It is only as the mind locates each idea within a domain of ideas, and locates their relationship to one another, that the act of cognitive discovery of an individual universal physical principle assumes the quality of a *distinct idea.*

It should be emphasized, as a point of clarification, that most universal principles of physical science are known to us today by the name of the putative discoverer. The student who has relived the original discoverer's experience, has thus reenacted the cognitive generation of the relevant hypothesis, as if that student had been the original discoverer. The student may, thus, reenact the experimental validation of that hypothesis, and thus rightly claim to know, rather than have merely *learned* (like a trained parrot, or a mere dupe of contemporary "information theory") the principle involved.

These features of a moment of Classical humanist education in acquiring knowledge of scientific principles, become generalized through the student's repeating the same kind of reenactment for other discoveries. The social relations among that panoply of discoverers, and the student's personal relationship to them and their

work, through cognition (e.g., Classical humanist methods of education), define a multiply-connected manifold of distinct ideas in the cultivated mind of the well-educated graduate.

The essential fallacy of the Hobbesian view of society as a collection of "interacting particles," should be obvious from the standpoint I have just summarized.

Since the progress of the human condition is the distinction of the existence of the human species, the natural relations within society are cognitive relations of the type just illustrated, in the foregoing discussion of transmission of those cognitive qualities of ideas, which correspond to elements of an integrated plenum of valid universal physical principles. It is such ideas, which are transmitted as a living form of idea over even thousands of intervening years, which express the characteristic of the natural form of human relations. It is this quality of relationship, not that of kinematically interacting Hobbesian particles, which defines the reality which the term *society* ought to connote.

Modern Suburban Savages

The difficulty which the foregoing remarks pose for most people today, should not be considered evidence that what I have just described suffers a fault of abstruseness. Rather, the resistance to my argument reflects the fact, that the existing forms of practice in today's prevalent culture, work to the effort of aborting the natural cognitive powers of the human individual in today's society. To state that point more vividly, but without exaggeration, we should reference the more typical U.S. suburbanite from the upper twenty percentile of the nation's family-income brackets. If not physically, then emotionally and cognitively, an increasing fraction of this stratum today is virtually "brain-damaged," hopefully, not beyond remedy.

Generically, the problem is an old one in type. The causes fall under two headings.

First, there is the need for a certain natural fostering of the cognitive and emotional development of the new individual, through the successive phases of infancy, childhood, adolescence, and young adulthood. This represents a period of approximately a quarter-century, from birth, to a mid-twenties level of potential young-adult maturity. An inadequate, or misdirected approach to the development of the young person during those successive phases, such as an abandonment of principles of Classical humanist education, may cause crippling

---

40. I.e., in Plato, higher hypothesis.

Certain oligarchies have decided not to educate young people "to imagine themselves above the social status to which we intend to degrade them. Promise them everything, but fill them with gin—or marijuana, or cocaine, or non-stop, dumbed-down forms of popular entertainment."

damage to that personality, presenting us the infantile child or adolescent, the childish, or even dangerously, emotionally infantile adolescent or adult, and so on.

Second, there is the factor of the willful damage to the cognitive powers of the maturing individual, imposed by certain oligarchies, and families, as a way of dumbing-down those more numerous members of society, who are intended, by current policy of practice, to be herded, by the methods of George Orwell's "Big Brother," into the status of virtual human cattle. (E.g., "Let us not educate young people above the level of the employment with which we destine them to be occupied." "Let us not educate them to imagine themselves above the social status to which we intend to degrade them. Promise them everything, but fill them with gin—or marijuana, or cocaine, or non-stop, dumbed-down forms of popular entertainment.")

The folly of mankind in general, is chiefly the result of a combination of those two methods, of negligence or willful malice, for aborting the redeemable goodness which exists as innate potential within each newborn individual person.

The orchestration of public opinion, as by the Webbs and others of the British Fabian Society, and by the American Fabian Walter Lippmann's prescription, typify the mechanisms which have been employed in the effort to degrade the U.S.'s so-called "middle class" and others, into a condition which, in effect, degrades them politically, intellectually, into the social status of virtual human cattle. This tactic of "dumbing down" the mass of the human herd, as by aid of today's popular mass-culture, is sometimes praised, by malicious ideologues, as a popular virtue of "other-directedness." One should remember those human cattle, called the citizens of Rome, marching into their seats within the arena, where they, the paragons of *vox populi,* the mass of Roman predators,[41] would drool with pleasure at the sight of lions killing and eating Christians.

That, essentially, was the social doctrine of Francis Bacon, Hobbes, John Locke, Bernard de Mandeville, François Quesnay, David Hume, Adam Smith, Jeremy Bentham, et al. That was the aesthetics of Kant, the doctrine of law of Hegel's confederate Savigny, the principle of the Nazi Nuremberg rally, of the recent motion-picture spectacular "Gladiator," and the Romantic doctrine of law of the Twentieth-Century neo-Hegelian fanatic Carl Schmitt.

The functional significance of what I have just underlined, is shown by comparing a Classical-humanist school room, in which the pupils relive the cognitive experience of original discoveries of valid principle, with the type of classroom in which students rehearse the expression of those opinions which they are instructed to regard as authoritative opinion. In the latter case, the brutish sort of teacher or parent, will warn the student, "When you have graduated from college, then

---

41. As I have emphasized, repeatedly, in earlier locations, the Latin term *popular* has the intentional connotation of "the predators," the class of Roman subjects whose chief function was to conquer, loot, or even exterminate other cultures, especially superior ones such as Hellenistic culture. The first modern fascist, the Consul and Emperor Napoleon Bonaparte, typifies the conscious use of the pagan Roman tradition in law and other institutions to create the kind of Caesarian society of the predators, which Napoleon established as the model to be imitated by Napoleon III, Mussolini, Hitler, et al.

you should think for yourself; in the meantime, in this classroom, you will learn to think and speak as I tell you." Or, a surly parent menacing his child, "When you grow up, you can think for yourself; in the meantime, you will believe what I tell you to believe!" Not surprisingly, the usual victim of such rearing reaches the age of twenty-five, or so, having successfully lost the greater part of his, or her innate potential to actually think cognitively, creatively.[42]

Thus, wherever the principle of Classical humanist education does not prevail, the student is conditioned to react in ways which conform to generally accepted classroom, or similar standards of social prejudice and teaching.

The case of that fraudulent description of Kepler's discoveries, associated with the admirers of Newton, is typical. Anyone who had actually worked through the documentation of those discoveries, step by step, could not be taken in. Why, then, are so many otherwise more or less distinguished scientists taken in by that Newton hoax? Simply, because it is the generally accepted classroom mathematical outlook, toward which they make fearful obeisance, for the sake of their careers and reputations among their peers. That typifies the way in which the brainwashing works.

That perversion of the all too typical contemporary classroom, is repeated, in most family households, in places of employment, and in the domain of general expression of what passes for opinion. The majority of today's under-fifty-five university graduates, typify the suburbanite fads of substituting perceived authoritative opinion, for thinking. The tyranny of popular opinion, as the lemming-like financial suicide of so many who have plunged into the market, typifies this syndrome.

This problem has been aggravated by the sympathy afforded to such degenerates as the late Theodor Adorno and Hannah Arendt. This exemplary pair of existentialist, anti-civilization fanatics, have been used to popularize their cult of hatred against persons they target as representing "the authoritarian personality."[43] Arendt, for example, premised much of her claim to academic achievement, on her mimicking of both her Nazi friend, Jean-Paul Sartre's Martin Heidegger, and Karl Jaspers, in promoting what was presently explicitly as a pro-Kant denial of the existence of truth. The result is equivalent to the kind of "Big Brother" syndrome of mass lunacy portrayed by George Orwell's *1984.* Those who follow such creatures as Adorno and Arendt in their abhorrence of truth, will therefore function in their relations toward other persons as do all true existentialists, as Friedrich Nietzsche did, like hungry rats in a crowded cage.

In the healthy development of the young individual, it is the fostering of the development of the cognitive potential of the infant, child, and adolescent, at every level, which is of paramount importance to family, schools, and society in general. The premium is on development of the child's and adolescent's capacity to discover truthfulness, to develop a sense of truthfulness as a inward source of personal identity and authority in society.

The root from which depraved existentialists such as Adorno, Heidegger, Arendt, Sartre, Frantz Fanon, et al., acquired their tradition, was, most immediately the legacy of pagan Rome, or, what is known in modern European history and culture as *Romanticism.* The denial of truth, in favor of caprices of public opinion, as the mob in the Colosseum typifies this, is characteristic of what is known to history as the oligarchical model, the model adopted by European feudalism, promoted by imperial Venice, and continued by the British monarchy to the present day.

The ugly fact about pre-modern forms of society, is that they were, at least predominantly, oligarchical models, in which the relative few, as a ruling caste or oligarchy, treated the majority of humanity as simply wild prey to be hunted, or as virtual human cattle. This is the predominant cultural feature of all known society prior to Europe's Fifteenth-Century Renaissance, even societies which contributed from within them, some of the most precious contributions humanity today enjoys from earlier times. Do not look for noble savages and their cultures in so-called primitive societies; none are evident, except in the childish fantasies of the credulous. The characteristic faults, moral and otherwise, of present-day, globally extended European culture, are the rotten fruit bequeathed to modern culture by ancient and medieval cultures, all of which were predominantly, viciously examples of the oligarchical model.

The moral and intellectual decadence, on these ac-

---

42. Psychiatrist Dr. Lawrence S. Kubie studied what he termed "the neurotic distortion of the creative process," and applied that study to the specific case of the pattern of cognitive sterility erupting in formerly gifted students at a point proximate to gaining a terminal degree. Hence, the often ironical implications of the academic term, "terminal degree." Lawrence S. Kubie, "The Fostering of Scientific Creativity," *Daedalus*, Spring 1962.

43. T.W. Adorno et al., *The Authoritarian Personality* (New York: Harper, 1950).

counts, of recent generations of young American victims of these trends, must take into account the moral effects of pattern-shifts in the quality of both employment, and of education for employment, especially during the recent thirty-five years.

During the immediate post-war period, there erupted a tendency for disdain for "blue collar" careers, which was expressed in the coordinated emergence of post-war suburbia and of related fads described, during the 1950s, as "White Collar" and "The Organization Man." Even in the relatively healthy side of this trend, there was a shift away from the identity of the scientist, to that of the engineer, and a related moral degeneration in the quality of engineering training, expressed by hostility to Classical artistic and related studies and concerns.

These and related trends in the national culture transmitted to the post-war generations, represented a shift away from earlier emphasis on the "rugged individual," whose sense of identity in acquiring knowledge and doing work, was one's own "inner-directed" development as a citizen, implicitly equal in moral sense of social status, even to those who held greater relative authority in political and economic life, and so on. The shifts into what I have emphasized as the new-suburbia trends in decadence of the post-war generations experience, represented a political and moral down-shift in the sense of the personal identity, from that of often poorly paid, but proud citizen, to the person whose crippled,"other-directed" sense of identity, is that of the menial lackey, even lackeys, such as our present-day Talleyrands and Fouches, who may have recently risen, if only temporarily, to levels of incomes in the order of millions of dollars.

"Who you are," became less significant, and what your relative status as a lackey might be, took over the world-outlook of the younger generations, more and more, especially during the recent thirty-five years.

The Cost of Mediocrity

All viable human cultures are characterized by growing populations. Only catastrophes, either natural or man-made, produce any different result. Whenever the collapse of life-expectancies or population-growth is caused by the society itself, rather than external interventions, the determining factor is a triumph of a type of mediocrity akin to that which has been spreading, like a cancer, in Europe and the Americas during the recent thirty-odd years.

The typical cause for all the catastrophes which a culture has brought upon itself, is the mass phenomenon known to Europe, since the literature of ancient Greece, as *the oligarchical model.* The recent thirty-five years' increasingly widespread and virulent cultural degeneration of the U.S.A. and European populations, typifies the way in which a culture may drag itself to the brink of even threatened extinction. The referenced example of what has happened to the U.S. suburbanite "Baby Boomer" stratum and its offspring, contains some of the most relevant evidence to this effect.

What we know of principles underlying such patterns, is learned chiefly from study of the evidence of the emergence of historical societies in the aftermath of the last great, cyclical melting of the glaciation of great portions of the Northern Hemisphere, a glaciation now approaching, in its customary timely way, once again, unless our development of science enables us to prevent that calamitous effect. What we know that is relevant to the matter before us here, respecting the emergence of mankind from the post-glacial period to date, is fairly summarized as follows.

The highest levels of development of those cultures known to us, present us with calendars and other products of relatively great transoceanic maritime cultures which developed during the millenia preceding the melting of the last great glaciation of the Northern Hemisphere. The characteristics of the relevant, most developed such calendars, are those which contain crucially significant characteristics of transoceanic maritime cultures. We know that the emergence of post-glaciation civilization, and of the cultures which produced it, were concentrated either in coastal areas, or through penetration inland along the course of principal large river-systems.

Typical is the transoceanic culture which dominated much of the development of the Mediterranean littoral, including its great influence on Egypt, and, the relatively inferior culture which developed in Mesopotamia, through the colonization of southern Mesopotamia by the maritime culture of that Dravidian-speaking set of colonizers, the "black-headed people" who founded Sumer.

As the case of the Egypt of the period of the building of the great pyramids attests, some of these cultures attained a high level of technological achievement, and yet they fell, repeatedly, into what appears to have been cyclical collapses into relative barbarism and collapse of population-levels, even on "dark age" scales.

This pattern is echoed in richer detail of its records

in more recent historical periods of ancient and medieval societies. Most relevant is the fact, the net effect of both Latin Rome's and Byzantium's culture, was a pattern of catastrophic decline in the level of Mediterranean culture, relative to the higher level of culture represented by Classical Greece and its influence on Hellenistic society prior to the crushing of the Greek states of southern Italy.

The general pattern of decay of Latin Rome and Byzantium alike, was reversed by the coincidence of the Abassid Caliphate in the East and Charlemagne in the West, and by the expression of the Augustinian tradition in the great cathedral-builders associated with Chartres, or the developments under Barbarossa, Frederick II, and Alfonso Sabio; but, the legacy of Rome, Byzantium, and the rising imperial maritime power of Venice, imposed recurring disasters, even dark ages, for the culture of medieval Europe and the adjoining Mediterranean littoral.

Even after the founding of the modern sovereign form of nation-state, during the course of the Fifteenth-Century Renaissance, the contest between, on the one side, the oligarchical model, typified today by the British monarchy and its influence over Anglo-American power, and, on the opposing side, the tradition of the American Revolution's model of sovereign nation-state republic, has been the characteristic struggle between the relics of the oligarchical and republican models throughout the recent five centuries.

All of the great tribulations of modern globally extended European civilization, are to be attributed chiefly to the role of the oligarchical model, and the impact of this degeneration within Europe upon other regions of the planet.

Throughout all of the known prehistory and history so just referenced above, the crucially determining feature of society's existence, has been the impact of the persistence of the oligarchical model. By "oligarchical model," we should understand, an arrangement, under which a relatively small portion of mankind, called an oligarchy or a caste, rules over a majority of mankind which is degraded to the condition of wild and hunted, or herded, bred, and culled, always as virtual human cattle. The ruling oligarchy exerts its power through the instruments of associated armed and other lackeys.

Only playful children would track deer, or herd cattle, out of zeal for enjoying conversation with either. Cattle who are more intelligent, saner than their peers, are said by those holding a shareholder interest in cattle,

to be too smart for their own good.

Typical of the point, are those provision of the Roman imperial Code of Diocletian, which is fairly described in modern terms as a malthusian population doctrine. Thus, just as the collapse of Latin Rome was chiefly the fruit of slavery's effect on the population, and its fertility as a whole, so Byzantium, which had survived for a time because of the superiority of its demographic characteristics and Greek culture, died for the same reasons of self-depopulation built into such customs as the Code of Diocletian.

In both examples, the combination of population policies like those of modern malthusians, and the dumbing down of the majority retained as virtual human cattle, as has been done by U.S. mass-cultural innovations of the recent thirty-five years, resulted in a lowering of the *potential* demographic and physical economic levels of the population per capita and per square kilometer.

Similarly, it was the anti-nation-state, globalization and usury policies of the Venetian maritime power and its Norman allies which, over a period from shortly after the Fourth Crusade to a hundred years later, plunged Europe into the great economic, cultural, and demographic decline, culminating in the New Dark Age of the Fourteenth Century.

The significance of the panoramic view I have just described, becomes clearer, when we take into account some of the great known contributions to knowledge and technology supplied from within some of the cultures otherwise self-doomed to collapse. That irony points up the fact, that even a culture which produces greatness from within part of itself, may be also self-doomed, that because of its suppression of the cognitive potentials and sense of political identity of the mass of its population. Thus, the recent two generations trends in U.S. policies of public and higher education, typify the contributing causes for both the present global economic collapse in progress and the recently ongoing moral, and intellectual degeneration of the population and its leading political parties and mass media.

The effect of the oligarchical model, in all its manifestations, including the post-World War II "suburbanization" of the U.S. culture, to which I have referred above, is to dehumanize the great majority of the population, actions which suppress the cognitive development of the population at large, and, thus, depress the ability of the economy to continue to meet the requirements of maintaining that culture.

In the typical of past cultures, there is a repression of that cognitive cultural development upon which the maintenance of the potential relative population-density of the culture depends. Thus, even though some parts of the culture's intelligentsia may make fundamental contributions to the perpetuation and improvement of available knowledge, the lack of participation in the acquisition and practice of knowledge by a "zero-growth" form of social culture, brings the continued existence of that culture into conflict with its own self-imposed ecological boundaries.

Thus, to maintain a submissive majority of the population, the cognitive development of that majority must be forcefully suppressed, as the Code of Diocletian specifies relevant measures to this effect, and as feudalism continued that Code's practice in such forms as the systems of serfdom and guilds. It was under such leading policies of Byzantium, Venice, and "globalizing" tendencies within feudalism generally, that the natural impulses toward the emergence of modern nation-states were suppressed, as this is typified by the brutish wars against the Holy Roman Empire's Frederick II and the efforts to eradicate the legacy of Alfonso Sabio in Spain, and the brutish conduct of Richard II, the brutish campaign of the Normans against France's martyred Jeanne d'Arc, and, later, the typically Norman evil of Richard III, in England.

The great net advances in the conditions of life of the human population on this planet, effected within modern European civilization, over the course of the interval circa 1400-1901, have been the result of the impulse supplied by the introduction of the modern sovereign form of nation-state, under France's Louis XI and his follower England's Henry VII. The principled source of this improvement is the introduction of a revolutionary new conception of statecraft, called the principle of the general welfare. Every evil experienced by, or caused by globally extended modern European civilization since, has been caused by the opponents of that constitutional principle.

Notably, the direct forerunners of that great Fifteenth-Century revolution, which is called the Renaissance, were the great educators, such as Abelard of Paris, Dante Alighieri, the Augustinian teaching order, certain Franciscans working to similar effects, the work of Dante's great follower Petrarch, and the exemplary great teaching order known as the Brothers of the Common Life. The characteristic of that great work, as Cardinal Nicholas of Cusa typifies the extension of this into the form of the Fifteenth-Century Renaissance, was the adolescent pupils' reliving the cognitive experience reflected, chiefly, in the great Classical Greek legacy, from which all of the great achievements of European civilization as such have fallen to mankind since. The role of Cusa in founding modern experimental physical science, with his *De Docta Ignorantia,* and the role of his self-designated followers, such as Luca Pacioli, Leonardo da Vinci, England's Gilbert, and Kepler, typifies the historical process.

Admittedly, since that time of the great Fifteenth-Century Renaissance, globally extended modern European civilization, has been a battlefield between those forces of the modern sovereign nation-state, and its general-welfare principle, and the oligarchical model most significantly typified, over these centuries, first, by imperial maritime power of financier-oligarchical Venice, and later the transfer of that role of Venice to the global, financier-oligarchical maritime power of Venice's chosen heirs, successively the oligarchs of Portugal, Spain, the Netherlands, and London.

However, that division within modern European civilization only defines the issue of principle the more clearly. The issue is the conflict between the principle of the sovereign nation-state, the principle of

EIRNS

Jeanne d'Arc walked in the pathway of Christ, losing her life, not through a tragic flaw, but for a sublime higher purpose.

the general welfare, and, its opponent, the infinitely murderous, financier-oligarchical, imperial interest expressed by the Anglo-American financier tyranny of today.

Thus, in history of the U.S.A., all of the important political struggles, including the internal struggle against the slave-system, has been a reflection of this conflict between the principle of the sovereign nation-state and the London-centered international financier oligarchy. The central expression of the issue of principle, has been that established by the Fifteenth-Century revolutionary change in political institutions, the establishment of *a sovereign nation-state whose fundamental law is that the moral authority of government is conditional upon its efficient promotion of the general welfare of all of the people and their posterity.*

The issue of Classical education, as education bears upon political and economic practice, is the central expression of the principle of the general welfare. Do we educate our young as cognitive beings, or do we develop them as virtually human cattle? Do we develop, or suppress the development of the cognitive potential within them, which sets human beings apart from lower forms of life?

The perpetual consequence of the kinds of policies of education, culture, and economic practice, of the U.S. during the recent thirty-five years trend, has been to degrade the cultivation and expression of the cognitive potential of our young, to a state corresponding to a self-doomed culture of virtual human cattle. Such has been the cost of the rampant mediocrity expressed in the economic and financial trends leading into the present systemic crisis of the system as a whole.

The pattern of the recent thirty-five years, since approximately the time of Richard Nixon's 1966 launching of his neo-Confederacy "Southern Strategy" campaign for President, has been the systematic destruction of the productive, educational, and infrastructural basis for a healthy society. Not only have the conditions of life of those in the lower eighty percentile of. family-income brackets been looted; the means for providing such employment, income, and standards of the general welfare, have been ripped up, by measures typified by the Nixon Administration's 1971-1973 campaign to nullify the Hill-Burton health-care law, and replace it with the predatory HMO policy.

Friedrich von Hayek's followers have thus achieved, in correspondingly great degree, the true, never really secret ambition of that co-founder of the Mont Pelerin Society, the return of globally extended European civilization, from civilization to serfdom. The fact that so many fools exist, in addition to Senator Phil Gramm, who admire Britain's Margaret Thatcher, who have embraced Mont Pelerin's neo-feudalist philosophy, is to be considered as one of the costs of the widespread mediocrity. Only mediocre, or very cruel minds could be taken in by von Hayek's perverse use of the term "freedom."

Thus, the U.S., among other modern nation-states of European civilization, has condemned itself to the same kind of oligarchical cycles which are typified by the rise and inevitable doom of the relatively powerful empires of the past. We are being destroyed, by ourselves, because we have allowed our children to adopt the intention that we be destroyed. That intention, is the cultural world-outlook which has prevailed in the U.S., increasingly, during the recent thirty-five years. That intention is most clearly expressed by the way in which we educate, entertain, and employ the future and present members of the labor-force and the members of their households.

The Cost of Classical Culture

I have thus indicated the negative features of the process. I conclude this section of the report with a summary of the positive factors to be considered.

Physical economy, as I have addressed that here thus far, is essentially the development of the power of the individual human mind to act in ways which increase mankind's power to exist in the universe. This power is found in the interdependency among chiefly several leading, contributing elements. I list each of those on which attention is concentrated here.

First, there is the quality on which I have already focussed here, the role of the cognitive powers of mind, in generating and communicating validated universal principles as solutions for otherwise insoluble ontological paradoxes of man's relationship to the "physical universe" so-called. So far, in this report, I have emphasized the discovery of those universal physical principles which bear on the per-capita relations of man to the physical universe.

Second, there is the first aspect of the social side of this power of the individual in the universe, the communication of not simply single valid principles, but a manifold of multiply-connected such principles, as Riemann's cited dissertation describes such a manifold: the ability of the individual to impart to and invoke in

"The issue of Classical education, as education bears upon political and economic practice, is the central expression of the principle of the general welfare." Here: David Heifetz of the Fairfax (Virginia) Symphony Orchestra rehearses with students.

other persons a specific sense of knowledge of distinct ideas.

Third, there is the class of universal principles which pertains to the processes of cognitive interactions among groups of members of society, and within society generally. In this case, we are studying social processes in the same general way we apply cognitive powers to discovering and conquering the ontological paradoxes encountered in our experience of the universe in which mankind exists. A competent study of economics, as from the standpoint of the science of physical economy, illustrates the existence of the same structure of multiply-connected principles, in the domain of social processes, as in man's conception of non-living and living processes.

Fourthly, there is the role of cognitive forms of motivation, as expressed by the sense of cognitive "fun" to which I have referred earlier. This is a quality of passion, as it spills over from the playfulness of the original discovery in science, a cognitive playfulness which is associated most closely with great works of Classical modes of artistic compositions, as in both plastic and non-plastic art-forms. It is this latter quality of passion which motivates us to dedicate ourselves, sometimes with overriding compulsion, to effects as much as a generation or more in the future. It is, therefore, this

aspect of the matter which is of special concern to us in the subsuming topic, long-range policy-planning, of this present report.

Although this latter quality of motivation is as characteristic of so-called physical scientific discovery as of great experiences in Classical art, it is in the greatest compositions and performances of Classical art that the significance of the passion is most immediately evident to explicitly social qualities of individual experience. The most relevant illustration of this point, is the Classical stage, as typified for our present purposes by the comparison of the great Classical Greek tragedies with the modern cases of Shakespeare and Friedrich Schiller. What is notable on that account, is the fact that the subject of that drama is politics, as situated historically. This latter connection serves us here, to emphasize both the importance of Classical art for fostering a rational basis for shaping the historical world-outlook of the mind of the statesman and citizen. Thus, as Classical tragedy illustrates most plainly, statecraft, and history, are situated under the reign of principles of Classical forms of artistic composition.

In several locations, within the present report as a whole, and in published writings earlier, I have emphasized the importance of the negative side of Classical drama, as typified by tragedy, and the positive complement to tragedy, which Schiller defined as the *sublime.* There is a point to be made on that account, at this immediate juncture.

Classical tragedy performs the indispensable function for society, of confronting society with its own propensity for bringing disaster upon itself. Through the great works of the Classical stage, tragedy shows us how entire cultures, acting under the influence of their leading institutions, such as a leading political figure, bring the entire society to an avoidable ruin, like the avoidable ruin under discussion in this present report. The positive side of tragedy, is that in a great performance of a well-composed work, the audience becomes aware of the fact that a willful alternative to doom existed in the case presented; the audience senses, thus, that if such a folly were to be encountered in some coming situation, that insight into the alternative to folly would provide society an escape from the type of calamity enacted on stage.

In the sublime alternative to tragedy as such, as in the case of France's Jeanne d'Arc, the cruel fate of the principal figure is not a subject of failure, but a triumph over evil. Without Jeanne's courageous commitment, to the end, France and the modern nation-state would not have come into actual existence, as it did because she had lived and acted as she had done.

This matter of the sublime, is no mere artistic elegance; it is an issue which confronts every sane person. We knew that we each were born, and shall die, sooner or later. Thus, it would be a tragedy indeed, if ours were such a society of fools as to think that individual self-interest lies in the kinds of hedonistic considerations listed by Adam Smith, as he argues for this in the passage I cited from his *The Theory of the Moral Sentiments.* Since we know that we all die, our interest in life is what we take out of it: For what should we spend that coin we call individual life, knowing that the meaning of our having existed will be nothing but what our living has given to the future? The rule of the wise person, is: *You have but one mortal life, spend it well; what you purchase will be the meaning of your existence for future mankind, throughout all eternity.* Only a person who lives so, is not intrinsically corrupt.

There lies the sublime, as the case of Jeanne d'Arc illustrates the point, both the Jeanne of history, and the Jeanne d'Arc as Schiller presents her on the stage. That is the passion which motivates all great Classical compositions, such as that of Johann Sebastian Bach and his anti-Romanticist followers, such as Mozart, Beethoven, Schubert, Mendelssohn, Schumann, and Brahms. It is so, as Brahms sets *I Corinthians* 13 to song. The passion so prompted, is that which Plato, and also the Apostle Paul, define as *agapē.*

This was the subject of an important essay, written by a great Massachusetts figure who was also a mentor of young Benjamin Franklin, Cotton Mather. Mather's injunction of the motive "to do good," expresses that passion which motivates the incorruptible ("inner directed") part of the scientific discoverer, the great artist, and the great statesman.

Economics as Classical Art

One of the greatest frauds commonly practiced today is the myth of objectivity. The myth is, that the hallmark of honesty is disinterest in the issue under consideration, and that lack of passion bespeaks a disinterested assessment of the impassioned issue at hand. "Sorry to kill you, fella'. Nothing personal; just doing my job," might the judge have said, when he condemned an entire section of the population to an increased morbidity rate, purely out of dispassionate regard for "shareholder interest." The only truly disinterested man is the "hanging" judge who, in matters of truth and justice, expresses the quality of disinterest otherwise shown by the female praying mantis, eating the head of the mate who is copulating with her.

It is the unfortunate consequences of an action, including actions of negligence, which deserved the passion which might have averted the calamity. Sometimes, it is indispensable not to avoid naming names; sometimes, on important issues, such as the career of Adolf Hitler, it is urgent to be very, very personal. In some cases, such as the genocide actually being willfully practiced throughout most of Africa, by known Anglo-American interests, such as those associated with London's Lynda Chalker, and formerly condoned by Secretary of State Madeleine Albright, the lack of passion is, in itself, an unspeakable crime.

Enough of tragedy; return to the sublime.

Take as an example, President Franklin Roosevelt's injunction respecting the awfulness of the situation produced by former President Coolidge's creation, the 1929-1933 Great Depression. So, today, it must be said: *We have nothing to fear as much as fear itself.*

The remedies exist, but they each and all depend upon predicating present action on confidence in a longer-term perspective. The use of the power of the sovereign nation-state to create national credit, is the indispensable means for organizing a process of general recovery from a catastrophe such as that of 1929-33, or the worse situation erupting today. This course of action depends upon mobilizing a passion in support of feasible programs which will not be self-sustaining in less than the medium to long term. On the basis of confidence in the prospect that such programs will become self-sustaining in their effects, government issues regulated credit to tide the nation and its people over, during the process of building up to a self-sustaining economic recovery.

The mustering of a combination of public and private credit for such medium- to long-term undertakings, requires the corresponding arousal of a passion for the future in a large part of the population, at least. A people will put up with much for quite some time, if three conditions are met. First, that the relative sacrifice is necessary; second, that the goal is credible; and, third, that we shall manage to get along decently, with gradual but significant improvement, in the meantime. Precisely that is required for the situation confronting the U.S. and its people, among others, today.

The great danger today, comes from the corrosive cultural influence of what is sometimes called "the now generation." This is the silly generation which tolerated the obscene delusion, that universities should not compel students to study the works of "dead white European males." The characteristics of the victims of such a mis-education, is that they are hostile to cognitive activity, and have no passion for the realities of either the past or the future. They are not future-oriented. In that sense and degree, they have no future, and the society which adopts their opinion will have no future, either.

This point is best illustrated by contrasting the quality of passion evoked by the qualified performance of a great tragedy, such as that of Shakespeare or Schiller, and the emotional response of the current rash of entertainments which substitute mere succession of sensual effects for a process of development. Even the pedestrian sorts of popular detective-story fiction from the 1930s through 1950s, contrast sharply with the gore-splattered-against-the-windshield sorts of TV crime-story productions today. To describe a film such as *Gladiator* as having some "redeeming" quality of plot, insults the imagination of anyone operating above the zombie-like level of an Nintendo-game addict.

It is only through those forms of communication which are best typified by Classical artistic composition, and study of statecraft and history in the same mode, that we muster the ability of a population and its leaders to respond with passion to the cause of bringing the future into being.

It is the great projects of nation-building and space exploration, which will motivate today's imperiled populations into reaching to the future as a way of rising from the otherwise insufferable conditions which grip the present.

4. The Sovereign Nation-State Economy

For anyone who is not ignorant of that revolutionary improvement in the demographic characteristics of human existence which was brought about through the Fifteenth-Century European creation of the modern nation-state, European civilization over the course of the recent six centuries has brought forth a degree of improvement in the human condition without precedent in all human existence before that time [**Figure 9**]. The causes for this success are encapsulated in the creation of a revolutionary form of state, one without actual precedent in any part of all human existence beforehand: the sovereign form of nation-state brought into being in the context defined by the great ecumenical Council of Florence, a Council whose leading organizers included the founder of modern experimental physical science, the later Cardinal, Nicholas of Cusa.[44]

The revolution which produced this new institution, the sovereign nation-state, is the point of origin of all modern economy.

What Cusa proposed in his **Concordantia Catholica,** echoing significantly the **De Monarchia** of Dante Alighieri,[45] can be fairly summarized by stating, that what he proposed was not a sovereign nation-state as such, but rather a system of sovereign nation-states, a system of the kind referenced later by then-U.S. Secretary of State John Quincy Adams, as a "community of principle." Cusa's grasp of the significance of the same notion of intention later echoed by his follower, Kepler, is of crucial significance for understanding the practical considerations of principle involved.

From the standpoint of the considerations identified in this report thus far, the notion of promoting the general welfare, subsumes the notions of maintaining and improving an existing level of *anti-entropic potential* for the present and future population as a whole, and also the corresponding development of the basic eco-

---

44. For another view of the uniqueness of the Fifteenth-century founding of the modern sovereign nation-state, see Friedrich-August von der Heydte, *Der Moderne Kleinkrieg als wehrpolitisches und militärisches Phänomen*, 1972 (also published in English translation under the title *Modern Irregular Warfare in Defense Policy and as a Military Phenomenon* New York: New Benjamin Franklin House, 1986). For Cusa on science, the reference is, again, to his *De Docta Ignorantia.*
45. Nicolaus of Cusa, *The Catholic Concordance*, Paul E. Sigmund, trans. (Cambridge: Cambridge University Press, 1991).

Growth of European Population, Population-Density, and Life-Expectancy at Birth, Estimated for 100,000 B.C.–A.D. 1975

Alone among all other species, man's numerical increase is a function of increasing mastery over nature —increase of potential population-density—as reflected historically in the increase of actual population-density. In transforming his conditions of existence, man transforms himself. The transformation of the species itself is reflected in the increase of estimated life-expectancy over mankind's historical span. Such changes are primarily located in, and have accelerated over, the last six-hundred years of man's multi-thousand-year existence. Institutionalization of the conception of man as the living image of God the Creator during the Golden Renaissance, through the Renaissance creation of the sovereign nation-state, is the conceptual origin of the latter expansion of the potential which uniquely makes man what he is.

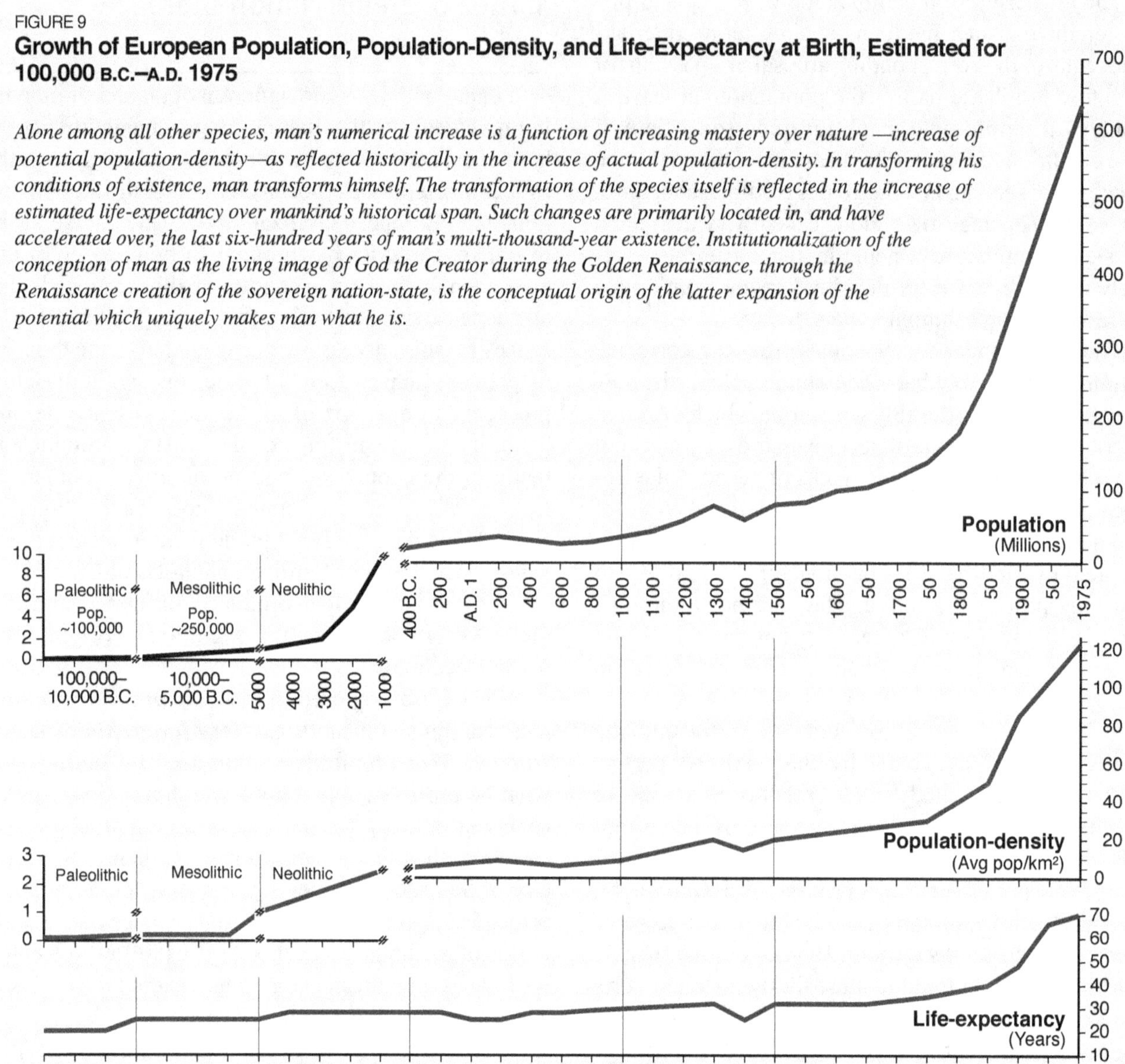

All charts are based on standard estimates compiled by existing schools of demography. None claim any more precision than the indicative; however, the scaling flattens out what might otherwise be locally, or even temporally, significant variation, reducing all thereby to the set of changes which is significant, independant of the quality of estimates and scaling of the graphs. Sources: For population and population-density, Colin McEvedy and Richard Jones, *Atlas of World Population History*; for life-expectancy, various studies in historical demography.

Note breaks and changes in scales.

nomic infrastructure of the society. This includes, prominently, the level of education and related development of the young and others in households. This requires the allocation of physical sources and protected conditions of individual and family life, for that population and the area of its habitation and other uses. These responsibilities imply real costs (as distinct from merely nominal, or money costs).

This means, in turn, setting the equivalent of wages and prices, per capita and per square kilometer, for the existence and functions which must be sustained in the interest of the general welfare. In effect, it becomes the responsibility of the government, under the principle of promotion of the general welfare, to foster protectionist regulation of costs and prices, and also to stipulate allocations for basic economic infrastructure, and some other things.

Under such arrangements, what is called the "market" is bounded by the way in which protection affects, chiefly, prices, costs, and certain priorities in allocation for basic economic infrastructure. The institution of these measures of protectionism, motivated by the principle of the general welfare, were the birth of modern economy. The complexities of European economy since that time, can not be understood, without reference to the indicated interdependency between the notions of protectionism and the promotion of the general welfare.

The First Nation-State

Elements of this complexity are to be seen in France's King Louis XI. The case of Louis XI, as the beneficiary of Jeanne d'Arc, serves us a double purpose here. We cite that case again, now, to make clear both a lesson from the panorama of history, and to make history clearer by means of a corresponding example from Classical artistic composition.

History is not a fiction practiced on the stage of a *tabula rasa.* This rule is clear in the process leading into Louis XI's coronation, and the circumstances under which he ruled thereafter. The case of Jeanne d'Arc, the intersection of her case with the reemergence of the Papacy during the decades immediately following her martyrdom, and the convergence of both her role and that of the outcome of the Council of Florence, are key to understanding how Louis XI came to power as he did. The mixed defeats and continued achievements of the circles of Cardinal Nicholas of Cusa, following that Council, were reflected in the increasing difficulties Louis XI and France suffered in the later part of his reign.

The history of Europe from the time of Venice's Fourth Crusade, near beginning of the Thirteenth Century, until the accession of England's Henry VII, was a nightmare, caused chiefly by the alliance of the imperial maritime power of Venice with the Norman interests largely controlling England and France, a legacy which continued to plague Europe into the time of the Fronde's alliance with France's Louis XIV.

The great New Dark Age which erupted during the middle of the Fourteenth Century, had begun with the wars against the Holy Roman Empire's Frederick II and his successors, during the middle decades of the Thirteenth Century, a war which had been continued through the so-called "Hundred Years War" and, in England, the "Wars of the Roses." Meanwhile, the fall of Constantinople had, for that time, ruined the ecumenical agreement reached during the Council of Florence, thus enabling Venice and its allies among the old Norman interests to reassert the authority lost during the earlier parts of the Fifteenth Century, leading thus into Venice's fomenting and orchestration of those religious wars of the 1511-1648 interval which threatened to eradicate the accomplishments of the Florence Council and Renaissance.

In this context, Jeanne d'Arc role played a crucial role, leading toward the liberation of France and the revival of the Catholic Church from the ruinous political strife of the Fourteenth and early Fifteenth Century. For that, her French and English Norman foes, the latter allied with a current anti-Pope, feared and hated her.

Although Friedrich Schiller uses a piece of fiction in dealing, on stage, with the issue used, in history, as a pretext for retrying and burning her, in transposing the events from the vast panorama of France to the pin-hole of the Classical stage, Schiller never deviates from the historical issue posed by the richly documented historical record of her case. On this account, Jeanne not only makes history, but serves as a vehicle for Schiller's efforts to lift drama from the relatively more primitive art of tragedy, to the higher Classical form of the sublime. As Bach's **St. John** and **St. Matthew Passions** use the New Testament to present Jesus Christ's mortal life and actions as the epitome of the sublime, so Jeanne walked in the pathway of Christ, losing her life, not through a tragic flaw, but for a sublime higher purpose, as Plato, earlier, had used the case of Socrates to assert the principle of the sublime, in contrast to the standpoint of the Classical Greek tragedians.

Thus, do real history and Classical artistic composition converge as one. Moreover, it was in the same setting of Jeanne's combat and martyrdom, that Cusa composed his ***Concordantia Catholica.***

The principle of the general welfare, as a principle of natural law, is the specification that no government has the moral authority to rule, except as it promotes efficiently the general welfare of the living and their posterity. The principle is more or less clear, from what we have considered in the preceding pages. However, that leaves a not-unimportant issue unresolved: *Who shall decide what promotes the general welfare? How shall that decision be judged? Who shall judge?*

The general answer to those questions, is fairly stated as reason. That means reason as defined by cognitive determination of truthfulness, in the Socratic sense of truthfulness, as all matters of universal principle must be defined in no other way. Who shall then judge whether or not, by reason, a government does, or does not meet the Gettysburg standard of *government of the people, by the people, and for the people? How shall the people know that they are being governed properly according to that principle?*

This points to a twofold issue posed by Dante Alighieri, the issue of Classical art. Since cognition occurs through the ironical use of language, the determination of the suitability of government must be made in terms of the language of the governed; however, that is not possible, if the language itself is not developed to the level of capacity for communication which such cognitive responsibilities imply. What shall then replace Latin as the language of government? Admittedly, within medieval Latin, the influence of Classical Greek had uplifted the use of Latin to a certain degree of literacy and related sophistication; but the problem of the use of language for government persisted. Thus, the pioneering by Dante and Petrarch founded the possibility of establishing the nation-state, as the reading of Dante's **Commedia** in the public places in Florence, show the pathway to elevating Italian into the condition needed for government according to reason.

Thus, for these and related reasons, it is clear that a nation must not be so small, a virtual micro-state, that it is not capable of a reasonable degree of sovereignty; but, we can not simply lump populations together, without a concurrence in the shared use of a literate form of language, a form of language conditioned to serve as a medium for cognitive communication.

The net result, is a system of nation-states, each immediately, and sovereignly responsible for its own general welfare, but, not indifferent to the general welfare among nations. So, there must be a standard of natural law, by which consenting nations agree to order their mutual relations in ways consistent with the promotion of the general welfare of each and all.

The Quality of the Citizen

The great affliction which threatens the best efforts of any modern statesman, is the persisting tendency of the great majority of the population to accept a self-policed status as a virtual herd of human cattle, rather than true citizens. Thus, in the recent U.S. Presidential election, the majority of those who voted, voted in the

FIGURE 10

America's Richest 20% Now Make More than the Other 80%

(percent)

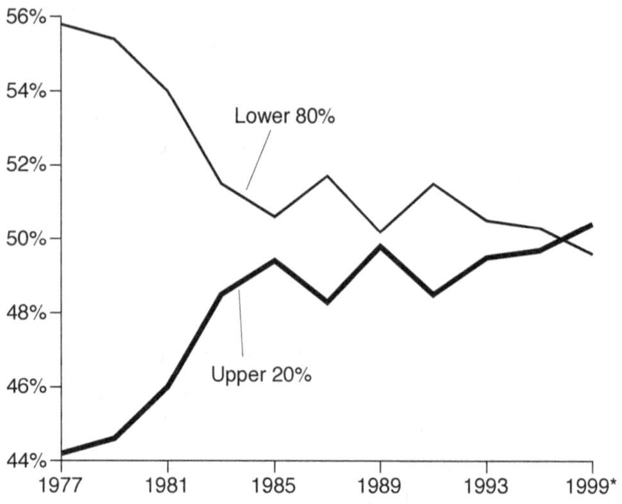

*Projected
Sources: Congressional Budget Office; *EIR*.

fashion of slaves begging for favors at the back-door of the master's mansion. They proposed to support a candidate, not because he was actually worthy of the office, but because they deluded themselves they might glean a favor or two from the one that they might not gain from the other. What was good for the nation, for their posterity, was, generally speaking, not their concern. They were like the slaves who said, "Master! We aren't asking for freedom; all we ask that you pay us off with a few shekels' worth of reparations." All for one measly, miserable bowl of pottage.

That state of mind of the generality of the U.S. adult population, is in itself a far step down from the temper of the same strata of the population thirty-five years earlier. The curve of the declining share of U.S. national income represented by the lower eighty percentile of the nation's family households [**Figure 10**], since President Carter's inauguration, shows the way in which the majority of the U.S. population has become accustomed to its economic and political degradation under the trend set by the Nixon "Southern Strategy" campaign of 1966-1968.

This decadence in the generality of the citizenry, is reflected in the moral degeneration of the educational system, in the degraded characteristics of what the population tolerates as popular entertainments.

The citizens of the U.S. have, in fact, the constitutional authority to free themselves from this oppression. They have reached the point they have temporarily lost the desire to do so. Better to be a fed pig in a pen, even if the butcher is not far off, than a beaten child in the master's house.

The responsibility of leadership, as long as society slides again, and again, into the habits of human cattle-likeness, is to awaken the people to their essential humanity. To arouse from the swinishness of Adam Smith's filthy doctrine, and to adopt a sense of mission which makes their life meaningful in the eyes of the Creator, meaningful in their own eyes.

The only method by which such attempts at leadership have succeeded, in the past 2,500-odd years of European civilization, is the method of Plato, the method which theologians sometimes term "spiritual exercises," as the referenced discoveries of Kepler typify such arousals of that in the individual which is made in the image of the Creator.

It is not with do's and don'ts, that the individual soul is saved. It is with a sense of mission, the mission of being, and acting as a creature made in the image of the Creator. That is the image which the true leader of a people must evoke from within those citizenry he seeks to uplift to rediscover their own true nature. That is the image of a true citizen of a true republic, which this republic of ours was founded to become.

5. Quarter-Century Cycles as a Standard of Accounting

As I wrote here of this paradox, in an earlier section of this report, in economics, the future lies in the present, and the success of the present is to be seen only in the mirror of its future. In practice, the future of immediate reference for the present, is a generation ahead, a period of approximately twenty-five years lapse of time, from today's newborn to the matured young adult of about twenty-five years.

For example, one to two generations, is the lapse of time which, in saner times, used to be required for a medium-income-level family household to acquire the ownership or equivalent of a suitable residence. Important infrastructure represents an investment in the same general magnitude.

Indeed, when we build a home, or equivalent housing, we should design and build it to last without disastrous costs of maintenance, for fifty to a hundred years or more: glorified tar-paper shacks with pasted-on Hollywood exteriors, at $400,000 and up, is not really the answer to the housing need, especially when a large ration of such speculative, low-grade, cheap-labor-built construction, has been dumped onto a market defined largely by the lately hired "new economy" recruits presently being dumped in droves. As might be recognized already, this aspect of the "Y2K"-keynoted, 1995-2000 "new economy" bubble, has not been particularly kind to the banks which have been involved in conducting credit into these not merely highly speculative, but even dubious markets. The way in which a new household formation brings forth a matured next generation, is thus a fair approximation of the span within which the making of the future must define the present.

Large-scale infrastructure, such as public utilities, educational institutions, should be designed with adaptation to new developments in mind, but the basic platform on which those new developments will be superimposed, should last for a quarter-century at least, and, with reasonable ratios of maintenance, better fifty to a hundred years.

Thus, for example, the idea of a wage can not be defined competently as the income paid to an individual. We must think in terms of household income, and of the conditions of household life needed to ensure the healthy production of the required quality of the next generation of the labor-force and its associated households. We must therefore think in terms of the conditions of life within the framework of that household, and associated extended families, and of the conditions of the community of which the household is a part. We must think of the organization of the living day in the household, including the hours in commuting daily, and of personal life associated with the household, as this bears upon such prominently included considerations as the rearing, and education of children and adolescents.

We must be alert to those errors in child-rearing and circumstances of childhood and adolescent life today, which tend to produce an impairment of the functional development of the individual who is presumably on the way toward adult maturity.

These and many considerations confronting us when we think approximately a generation ahead, usually involve cost, in some sense of cost to society. These costs must be paid, in one way or another. How shall we

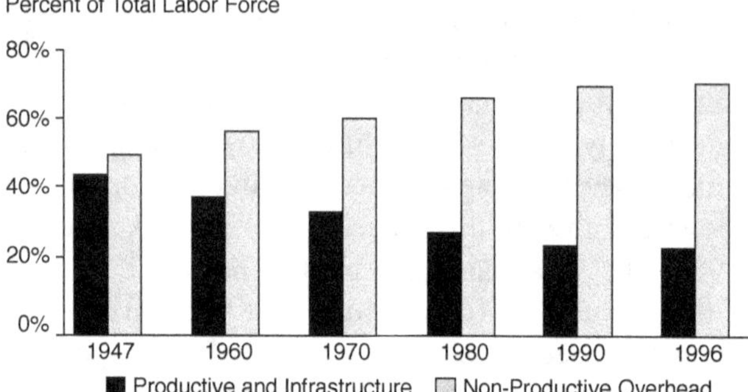

FIGURE 11

Productive Compared to Non-Productive Labor Force, U.S.A.

Percent of Total Labor Force

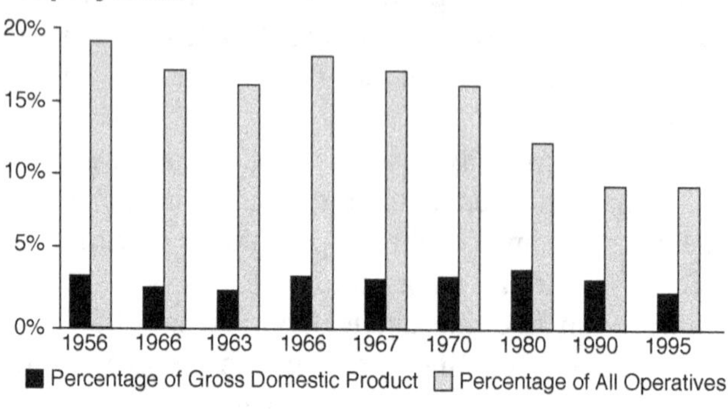

FIGURE 12

U.S. Manufacturing Investment and Employment

be able to pay?

For one thing, we must set certain priorities. Keep the unnecessary overhead down, for example. Generally, after all the relatively obvious measures of economy are taken into account, there remains a substantial deficit in what might be projected as available future income against morally unavoidable future physical costs. We must always think, first of all, in physical terms, rather than financial ones. Whence the additional margin of income?

In general, the answer to the question so posed, is scientific and technological progress. The question becomes: What programs of accelerated investment in scientific and technological progress will foster the rates of increase of the physical productive powers of labor needed to balance the implied budget of the economy overall?

The dull-witted sort of accountant, perhaps a fellow-traveller of Senator Phil Gramm, will answer "slash expenditures; we can not afford more investment in research and development at this time." The problem of the linear mentality, to which I have made frequent reference here already, has thus cropped up once again.

The solution to the problem is human in nature. The human being, if properly educated and inspired, is an ultimately inexhaustible source of creativity, as discovery of valid universal physical principles typifies this creativity. This creativity, so expressed, is characteristically anti-entropic. That is, the more we are able to spend for that anti-entropy, the greater the rate of growth of the real net national income.

The shaft of the spear of anti-entropic progress, is education combined with the fostering of Classical culture. However, to get the shaft through the target effi-ciently, we must put a sharp point on the spear. The best choice of point is what is called an economically broadly based "crash science-driver program," as typified by the pre-1966 phase of President Kennedy's manned Moon landing program.

I explain a few crucial points respecting such a much-needed "crash science-driver program" for the world today.

Reconstruction

Turn your attention to the categories of employment of the U.S. labor-force over the interval 1946-1965, prior to the injection of the pro-malthusian phase-shift of 1966-1967, into the U.S. Federal budget. Trace the decline of those categories of employment which had been associated with technologically-driven increases in development of basic economic infrastructure and physical production of physical goods, prior to 1966. Contrast this with the shift in composition of categories of total employment over the interval 1971-1987, and, again, the shift over the interval 1989-2000. [See **Figures 11** and **12**.]

Now consider reducing the percentiles of employment in services, by category, to the levels of 1946-1965. Then, intend to shift the percentile cut from employment to the effect of restoring the percentiles of composition of employment to levels consistent with 1946-1965 trends in composition of employment of the total labor-force. This means, in effect, the shift of composition of employment of the total labor-force, back to the more productive composition of the earlier, pre-1966 interval.

Since we are presently headed for massive unemployment, the kind of shift of composition of employ-

The most crucial thing, is to instill in the population an informed sense of mission for the future. Then, as Franklin Roosevelt said, we shall have nothing so much to fear from this new great world-wide depression, as fear itself. Here: President Roosevelt in 1936, with drought-stricken farmers.

ment indicated will be best accomplished simply by absorbing new employed into expanded employment in categories corresponding to the more physically productive component of employment. This means, of course, government programs, in the spirit of FDR's recovery effort, which steer credit into the categories of employment which are more desirable, because of their impact on the desired increase of the physical productivity of the labor-force as a whole.

This means, of course, much higher rates of Federal and other taxation on those relatively upper-bracket personal and business incomes which are not recycled as investments in the physically productive sectors of the economy. This would be added by reversing Kemp-Roth and related follies, to increase radically the financial capital-gains tax-rate, but with a compensating investment-tax-credit program along lines not dissimilar from President Kennedy's program.

The idea that increasing the ratio and amount of tax-free financial gains would promote productive investment, was a fairy-tale in the first place. The way to manage the job, is to reward those who employ their gains for the increase of physical productivity of the economy, and tax those relying upon speculative appreciations at the relatively highest rates. We must learn the lesson of thirty-odd years of liberal folly, recognize the mistakes of deregulation and the like, and restore what had worked before the ruinous effects of Nixon's and Carter's elections as President.

The leading edge for the initial mass of raw growth such a recovery program will set into motion, will be infrastructure. Here, my outline earlier of the implications of the infrastructural interface between mutual development of noösphere and biosphere, should predominate in policy-shaping. The increase of water throughput, energy throughput, and higher energy-flux densities, per capita and per square kilometer, chiefly through public utilities, will provide the initial leading stimulus for economic recovery in both infrastructure and those entrepreneurial activities affected by expansion of infrastructure.

This emphasis upon infrastructure, should build the platform for a two-fold approach to upgrading the productive powers of labor in the so-called private sector generally. In short, the two approaches are, respectively, bottom-up and top-down. Bottom-up, means the traditional approach of the 1939-1965 interval: upgrading the quality of employment of so-called "blue-collar" and other productive employment, with emphasis on technology-intensive, capital-intensive modes for bringing this effect about. Top-down, means a "crash science-driver program" approach, in which the mere development of scientific discovery is treated as the highest priority quality of product produced by the economy as a whole.

To situate the top-down aspect of the program, look at the global prospects for a U.S. long-term economic recovery.

U.S.-Eurasia Cooperation: Science as a Product

Among the crucial economic situations in the world at large, is the collapse of the export margins of the German economy, the economy on whose support the entirety of western continental Europe depends for its economic vitality. The natural export market for western continental Europe as a whole, is chiefly Eurasia. The pivot for any such cooperation between western continental Europe and Asia, is Russia. Relations among Russia, China, and India, are the keystone upon which broader cooperation in Asia depends more or less absolutely. It is through western continental European cooperation throughout Eurasia, in cooperation with Russia, that a general and durable economic recovery of Eurasia as a whole becomes feasible. In a rational state of affairs, the government of the U.S.A. would eagerly cooperate with its partners in western continental Europe in such a Eurasia undertaking.

This is not to deprecate the importance of Africa or of Central and South America, or of Australia and New Zealand either. Rather, unless the Eurasian land-mass pivot is viable, the world lacks the net resources to provide much-needed rescue for Central and South America, or Africa.

There are two economic fulcra in this Eurasia project. One is the underdeveloped landmass of Central and North Asia. The other, is the fact, that without massive infusion of technology into nations such as China and India, beyond the internal resources of those nations themselves, the amount of technology which could be infused into those two most populous nations would not be sufficient to overcome the burden of the deep impoverishment of the less developed portions of the populations and areas of those nations, in particular.

The solution for these and related challenges internal to Eurasia, is a long-term reorientation of the economies of the traditional technology-exporting nations of the world, toward the technology-hungry appetites of East, Southeast, and South Asia. Essentially, this means applying the lessons actually and implicitly learned from the 1946-1965 cooperation between the U.S.A. and western continental Europe, to the expanded horizons of Eurasia as a whole.

It would be a great mistake to imagine that such a program could succeed on the basis of off-the-shelf technologies from present U.S. and European enterprises. The degree of technological leverage represented by such inventories, is not sufficient to accomplish the implied mission in a timely degree. There must be a virtual explosion of scientific progress, and technological progress driven by scientific progress, to the effect of increasing the rate of technological gain greatly beyond that which would be possible with off-the-shelf-plus strategies.

This means, that the potential volcanoes of large-scale technology export, such as the U.S., western Europe, Russia, a resuscitated Korea, and Japan, must cooperate with other nations in creating a virtual new category of employment: "crash science-driver program" employment.

Realistically, such a program must come chiefly from national governments, mobilizing such a new industry on the basis for lessons from projects such as the Manhattan project and the post-war space programs. This means a heavily overloaded, ostensibly "overstaffed" initiative, not one conducted according to today's accountants' notions of efficiency. This means, heavy engagement of universities, with build-up of their science departments and research projects, with much emphasis on pre-benchmarking notions of engineering design for advanced experimental work.

It means the inclusion of such programs as the Sänger project's scramjet program, for lower-energy-cost access to geostationary Earth-orbit, and every other plausible avenue of task-oriented space-exploration work. It also means, a crash-program approach to the noösphere-biosphere concepts of Vernadsky et al, with much emphasis on the kinds of biophysics implied by that work, as opposed to the dubious claims for molecular biology's cure for practically anything.

The intended by-products of such a broadly defined "Vernadsky Project," should include new assistance to crop programs, aimed to secure the world's food supply, in both quantity and quality. It should include broader-based study of infectious and other diseases, and the possible remedies. It should emphasize helping the biosphere to transform wastelands into viable crop-lands and areas of habitation. It should include the build-up of useful, managed forests, as part of the build-up of the biosphere. It should foster improved approaches to developing long-term residential areas, public facility areas, and commerical and industrial areas, in ways which a deeper understanding of noösphere and biosphere suggest.

The most crucial thing in all of this, and related work, is to instill in the population an informed sense of mission, looking toward what must become a quarter-century ahead, and still further. Then, as Franklin Roosevelt said, we shall have nothing so much to fear from this new great world-wide depression, as fear itself.

For Further Reading

The following bibliography of recent articles provides extensive documentary and analytical material on subjects that are covered in this article by Lyndon LaRouche.

Jonathan Tennenbaum and Bruce Director, "How Gauss Determined the Orbit of Ceres," *Fidelio*, Vol. 7, No. 2, Summer 1998.

Lyndon, H. LaRouche, Jr., "New Accounting Systems Are Imperative: The Becoming Death of Systems Analysis," *EIR*, Vol. 27, No. 13, March 31, 2000.

"Any cost-conscious corporate management so reckless, as to imagine it might be permitted to reduce costs by substituting so-called mathematical modelers, for the type of design-engineering developed for the tasks of testing new universal physical principles, should be promptly discharged, that out of consideration for urgent issues of managerial incompetence."

LaRouche, "On a Basket of Hard Commodities: Trade Without Currency," *EIR*, Vol. 27, No. 30, Aug. 4, 2000.

"A basket of commodities ... is to be understood as a shared commitment to do good. The issue of economy is, therefore, not the exact price to be placed on any commodity, but the good will expressed in the way a reasonable estimate of a fair price is adopted. On that basis, a reasonable price for a unit basket of commodities, will be the right price in practice."

LaRouche, "The Lost Art of Management," *EIR*, Vol. 27, No. 35, Sept. 8, 2000.

LaRouche clarifies "what today's leaders must come to recognize as the deeper meaning which they ought to attribute to the term 'full set economy.'"

LaRouche, "Benchmarking: Faking as an Art of Self-Deception," *EIR*, Vol. 27, No. 42, Oct. 27, 2000.

The admission that the U.S. government has been faking its official inflation statistics, plus the surfacing of a letter in which Ford executives described how they covered up a design-failure in the firm's best-selling Sport Utility Vehicle, "tell us much, if not quite all, about the administrative reasons for the presently onrushing collapse of the global, Anglo-American-dominated financial system."

LaRouche, "A New Voyage to Laputa: California Takes a Swift Look at Today's Economists," *EIR*, Vol. 28, No. 5, Feb. 2, 2001.

Why have nearly all among today's ostensibly leading economists failed so miserably? The defective mentality behind their policy failures, is a pervasive cultural disease. Jonathan Swift's famous *Gulliver's Travels* suggests the explanation for the follies of today's middle-aged economic-policy Laputians.

LaRouche, "On the California Energy Crisis: As Seen and Said by the Salton Sea," *EIR*, Vol. 28, No. 7, Feb. 16, 2001.

Unless President George W. Bush abandons his present ways, his policies are now going to lead his administration toward a global crisis "so horrifying, that most of you would not now even try to imagine it.... For the sake of all of us, please permit me to lead you, step by step, into discovering for yourselves, what it is that you need to know, if we all are to work our way out of this mess."

LaRouche, "A Philosophy for Victory: Can We Change the Universe?" *EIR*, Vol. 28, No. 9, March 2, 2001.

Classical philosophy, properly defined, is the only branch of science in which possible solutions to the crisis in U.S. decision-making can be rationally discussed.

Vladimir Ivanovich Vernadsky, "Problems of Biogeochemistry II: On the Fundamental Material-Energetic Distinction Between Living and Nonliving Natural Bodies of the Biosphere," Jonathan Tennenbaum and Rachel Douglas, trans., *21st Century Science & Technology*, Vol. 13, No. 4, Winter 2000-2001. The first complete English translation of a 1938 article by the innovative Russian biogeochemist, who saw the human mind as the highest development of natural processes.